Into the Networked Age

How IBM and Other Firms Are Getting There Now

Into the Networked Age

How IBM and Other Firms Are Getting There Now

James W. Cortada
Thomas S. Hargraves
with Edward Wakin and an
IBM Team of Consultants

New York   Oxford
Oxford University Press
1999

Oxford University Press

Oxford New York
Athens Auckland Bangkok Bogotá Buenos Aires Calcutta
Cape Town Chennai Dar es Salaam Delhi Florence Hong Kong Istanbul
Karachi Kuala Lumpur Madrid Melbourne Mexico City Mumbai
Nairobi Paris São Paulo Singapore Taipei Tokyo Toronto Warsaw

and associated companies in
Berlin Ibadan

Published by Oxford University Press, Inc.
198 Madison Avenue, New York, New York 10016

Library of Congress Cataloging-in-Publication Data is available
ISBN: 0-19-512449-9

9 8 7 6 5 4 3 2 1

Printed in the United States of America
on acid-free paper

Contents

Foreword

Managing change in small and large enterprises is an essential competence all managers must have today. That observation is obvious and rarely challenged anymore. What is only just now becoming obvious, however, is the extent to which all firms have to change to remain profitable and successful in the years to come. Looking back on all the changes firms went through over the past decade gives us insight on what it means to our individual enterprises when an economy is moving from one historic era to another. We are experiencing the transition from the Second Industrial Age to a new economic order that many are calling the Information Age, but about which all managers are just learning. We already know, however, that to be successful in this transition calls for firms and government agencies to be nimble on their feet, quick to change processes, sharp in their ability to understand customers' needs and wants, and mentally prepared to accept new notions and to offer original services.

We have all learned that change is hard to do, takes too long, and is very complicated. IBM's experience is a case in point.

The general outline of IBM's journey over the past decade has only been partially told in public. We all know that IBM's traditional markets began to change in the late 1980s, that by the early 1990s the firm was not transforming fast enough from a traditional mainframe vendor to one capable of selling smaller products and services. But the firm recognized the need for changes, made them, and, as we sit poised at the start of a new millenium, this nearly century old firm feels young and energized. It is also growing profitably. Its growth is ideal because it is organic, not the result of acquisitions to gain scale; it is expansion caused by customer demand. Acquisitions have been made to gain capabilities that have translated into new offerings for our set of customers. How did all of these changes happen? You'll learn the answer to that in this book. Have lessons been learned that can be applied successfully in other enterprises? Has the competency of change been enhanced with new learning? At IBM we believe the answer to these questions is yes.

First, the firm is different from what it was. It has grown, enjoyed profitable years, and changed its mix of products and services. In the early 1990s, IBM hemorrhaged financially. After downsizing, repositioning its products, reorganizing several times, reengineering processes, and employees acquiring new skills during the middle years of the 1990s, the firm emerged very profitable and on a path of healthy revenue growth. The company went from approximately 85 percent of its revenues coming from sales of hardware in the late 1980s to today's mix in which over a third of our revenue comes from services, such as management consulting, running information technology assets for our customers, and implementing new software systems. The firm everyone at one time thought only sold mainframes changed in less than a half-decade to one of the world's largest service organizations.

Second, the story of IBM's renaissance is a model of how one could change the fundamentals of the business while keeping its doors open and still providing goods and services long the hallmark of the firm. One of the least known stories about our transformation concerns IBM Global Services. In 1991, the company decided to do what customers had been asking it to provide for over a decade: create a real consulting operation that could advise people about the best use of information technology, provide skills to install and operate technology, and to help enterprises through a professional management consulting organization. The delivery organizations put in place to carry out this mission were called the IBM Consulting Group (to do the management consulting) and ISSC (to perform technical services). The firm had little experience in some of these services (especially in classical management consulting) and, like its consulting competitors, had yet to realize how critical it would become to scale up in size and scope while remaining profitable. Between 1991 and the end of the decade, IBM created what we now call IBM Global Services, an organization that employs one-third of IBM's employees, generates approximately that same proportion of revenues, and brings together in one group a broad array of skills from pure management consulting to operating networks and data centers.

The experiences and insights gained from creating that new line of business, while simultaneously transforming the firm as a whole to reflect new market realities, generated a massive reservoir of skills, knowledge, methods, and cases of how to transform. Simultaneously, our consultants helped thousands of clients do the same thing in several dozen industries and around the world. Part of our success quite candidly came from the fact that as the IT content of many transformations increased, circumstances played to one of our core strengths—knowledge of information technology—making it possible to "get up to speed" with clients very quickly by delivering services and value at the rate at which we were all changing. But this was also a situation in which we applied lessons learned at IBM to client projects. We also took the time to learn from client experiences what we could do for ourselves and for other customers.

The result of these experiences is the content of this book. As the IBM team that wrote this book argues, you cannot just change, you have to reflect on that process to improve the inevitable next round of transformation required of all managers and their organizations. Because we are in a major historic transformation, bigger than any one company, the winners are going to be those that arrive at the new economic model before their rivals. The ability to do that requires becoming smarter about how to change. This book clearly explains what we have learned over the past decade. As the authors demonstrate, change is multifaceted, operates at various speeds, and in different ways within the same enterprise. It is organic and fluid, almost with a life of its own, but also the product of design and intent. The authors show us how to balance change that happens anyway with change that comes that you have shaped.

The title of the book suggests the profound influence technology is having on change. What we realize is that the root cause of many of the changes under way within both organizations and national economies are the result of technological innovations in digital technology, computing, software, and telecommunications. Hence the book's title. Yet we also have realized that while technology stimulates change, the basics of sound management must be applied across many nontechnical issues, ranging from process management and the leveraging of the firm's competencies to execution of visionary leadership that displays purpose and practical actions.

We encouraged the team that wrote this book to collect our internal experiences in a way that would help all managers with a method of learning a proven path to the Networked Age. The authors share one experience in common: they all helped IBM transform and helped clients do that as well, and always successfully. As their biographies suggest, this is a battle-tested team that knows as much about transforming an enterprise as you will find anywhere. They played important roles in both helping IBM and our customers, while codifying what we have learned, so their learnings could be shared with thousands of colleagues at IBM and our clients. Several are internationally recognized experts in various facets of transformation, sharing our insights with clients through speeches and publications.

I recommend this book to you as a convenient way to learn what we at IBM and so many of our customers have learned. It is logical, clearly thought out, and realistic. It is a reflection of how we will continue to transform at IBM. If there is one message to take away from this book, it is that change is a way of life now and that it can be managed and guided with the same confidence that you and I have in running other parts of an enterprise. There is a growing body of management "best practices" in change, which this team of authors has put together as a wise book for all of us to read. Learn their lessons and be part of the success story of the new Information Age.

Michael Albrecht, Jr.
General Manager,
IBM Consulting and Services, Americas

Preface

Managers have no choice. They must change not once, but continuously or suffer the consequences of losing out to the competition they already know or will confront—to their surprise. No easy response, single idea, or quick fix is the answer. Instead, one must develop an open-ended response that is equal to the task. Such a response is designed to keep up with and even stay ahead of change with a holistic approach that brings all change formulas and all resources, functions, and processes together. The operational expression of this holistic approach is teaming on the broadest possible enterprise level.

That, appropriately, is also the way this book has been written, not by committee but by a coordinated IBM team that has been there, that has done it, and that continues to do what is needed to cope with change that is itself changing. The members of the team are doing it not only within IBM, but with a range of clients across the full spectrum of industries in the United States and around the world. They draw on their track record, their know-how, and their accumulated experience.

The thinking behind what we present as a breakthrough book addresses the fundamental issues of how companies can transform themselves to compete in the new economic and business age. The stakes are survival: exploit emerging economic opportunities or rapidly wither away. The response revolves around open-ended transformation of the way firms operate and do business.

This book focuses on how corporations are evolving into enterprises capable of operating successfully in a post-industrial, global economy. These organizations confront change that has itself changed during the 1990s. In less than a decade we have gone from reengineering organizations to holistic transformations, from stand-alone PCs on every fourth worker's desk in the industrialized world to the Internet, with a PC for nearly every worker in *Fortune* 1000 firms. We have gone from wondering if process management and quality are good ideas to operating flattened organizations with extensive employee empowerment in a process-centric environment. All of this in less than one decade.

IBM is one such organization that is successfully transforming itself. It has gone from a company with less than $60 billion in nearly unprofitable revenue (when reengineering was the rage) to a highly profitable, $85-billion-plus enterprise. It has gone from a firm whose major source of revenue was hardware to one in which services account for more than one-third of total revenues and in which half the employees do anything but sell computers. IBM Global Services, which was non-existent in 1992, has become a $25 billion organization—with almost all of its business coming from firms transforming themselves, as IBM has done. Not only have the IBM team members participating in this book taken part in and experienced radical change, they have also helped thousands of firms do the same. Why? Because many of the changes involved computing and the management of information: mainframes, client servers, PCs, networks, e-business, the Internet, data bases, knowledge and competency networks, and technical management.

Accordingly, the themes in this book are change-focused, as befits the one predictable and persistent reality of the globalized marketplace. Our themes are, simply stated:

- Change occurs fast.
- Change as a process also transforms over time.
- Change demands that firms keep up with their customers in the shift from a supply-side to a demand-side response and the accompanying rise of customer power.
- Change is effective when management exploits knowledge, follows a process-centric approach, and uses technology appropriately.

- Change in organizations succeeds if it is holistic, meaning it affects every aspect of the enterprise.

The parts of this book are organized around these issues, beginning with an examination of the nature of change based on several thousand cases the authors have researched or in which the authors have been directly involved. Because change has become a pervasive, complex phenomenon encompassing myriad parts, pieces, and specialties, no single individual can know enough to single-handedly provide a workable, thoroughly tested blueprint. Each member of the writing team has particular expertise that has gone to work in the successful transformation of firms in the United States and around the world. Each person has researched, written about, and applied transformation in all of its manifestations and ramifications: in how work is organized, how resources are used, how technology is applied, how customers are served.

Knowledge itself of transformation has changed. So much has been happening and so much has been learned that the knowledge of the early 1990s is already out-of-date. Whereas the early focus was on downsizing as manifested in the way reengineering was applied, the emphasis shifted to changing processes and growing the business. In a few short years, a new body of knowledge and experience has emerged. Today, firms that transform are better organized and better coordinated. They recognize transformation as a journey rather than a destination. What managers will find here is a guidebook that prepares them to remake their companies and to continue remaking them—transforming them.

Lessons from the IBM turnaround and the client experiences of its consultants show how companies are redesigning themselves today in distinctive ways that reflect their history, leadership, resources, competition, and industry, as well as global forces. As distinctive as individual case studies are, there are universals in deciding upon strategies and tactics. Transformation is holistic, process-centric, knowledge-based, and technology-driven.

Company management teams need to connect strategy and tactics, to match what they offer to what customers want, to change within to keep pace with change without. They need to identify and activate core competencies that put them ahead of the competition. Companies that anticipate change and reinvent themselves become open-ended. They develop the capacity to transform themselves on an ongoing basis. They apply the fundamental lesson of success today and tomorrow: continuous change rationally implemented.

We would like to take this opportunity to thank the many individuals who helped us with this book. At IBM, senior executives endorsed and supported this project: Michael Albrecht, Paul Lewis, Gregory D. Wyllie. Each chapter reflects the thinking of hundreds of IBM colleagues connected to each other through competencies organized around such issues as process management, organization, change management, and IT strategy. They all contributed intellectual content to this book. Jeffrey Modjeski designed the art work, taking our notions and turning them into graphics that helped explain our messages. Ping Chow acted as our venture capitalist in supplying us funds with which to write this book, confident that the investment would be worth it.

At Oxford University Press we owe a profound debt of gratitude to our editor, Herbert J. Addison. He brought decades' worth of experience to the project, constantly mentoring us, while insisting on clarity of thinking. Then he published the book.We also would like to acknowledge the high professionalism displayed by CWL Publishing Enterprises, which designed the book and produced it in 50 percent less time than is normal in the publishing industry. Finally, we want to acknowledge the help of Peter Vogt, our copyeditor, who helped us polish our text.

James W. Cortada
Thomas S. Hargraves

About the Authors: The IBM Team

This book was written by a team from IBM. In order to cover the broad range of topics required to deliver the central theme of the book—that ongoing corporate growth and transformation require a holistic approach, and thus the use of a wide variety of colleagues working as a team—we too needed to practice what we were describing. It is the way we work at IBM. Your IBM team comprises a broad collection of skills, knowledge, and experiences without which this book would have been impossible to write.

James W. Cortada is an Executive Consultant within IBM Global Services. He consults in the area of business transformation. He has designed processes for sales, marketing, utility industry functions, and corporate cultural transformation. He is a leading expert on quality management practices and best practices in Information Technology. He has been with IBM in a variety of sales, marketing, management, and consulting roles for 25 years.

Jim is the author of several dozen books and nearly one hundred articles on such topics as IT best practices, quality and process management, and knowledge management. His most recent books include *Best Practices in Information Technology* (Prentice Hall, 1998) and *Rise of the Knowledge Worker* (Butterworth-Heinemann, 1998). He is also the co-editor of *The Knowledge Management Yearbook* (Butterworth-Heinemann). He is currently collaborating with a team of scholars on *The Information Age in Historical Perspective*, to be published by Oxford University Press in 2000.

Jim attended Randolph-Macon College and holds an M.A. and a Ph.D. in history from Florida State University. He is a member of the American Society for Quality and the American Historical Association, and he is the chairman of the Charles Babbage Institute at the University of Minnesota. You can reach him at: jwcorta @us.ibm.com.

Thomas S. Hargraves is a Principal with IBM's Consulting Group in IBM Global Services. He specializes in assisting clients in business transformation strategies, process reengineering, and management systems and in quality improvement disciplines. He also is a major contributor to IBM's intellectual capital in the area of process management.

Tom has redesigned processes within IBM and within the utility, transportation, process and petroleum, and manufacturing industries. He played a crucial role as a member of the IBM team that developed much of the current intellectual capital on process management used by IBM consultants around the world. He also led IBM's Market Study Initiative, which identified and assessed all market and customer research throughout the corporation, contributing toward a corporate-wide segmentation strategy with an emphasis on customer value. He is a frequent speaker on the subject of process management at business conferences. Prior to joining IBM, he was a process and project engineer at Air Products and Chemicals, Inc., where he did process engineering, research, and development.

Tom holds a B.E. and an M.E. in chemical engineering from Manhattan College. He earned his M.B.A. in finance from the Lubin Graduate School of Business at Pace University. You can reach him at: tsh@us.ibm.com.

Eric L. Lesser is an Executive Consultant with the IBM Consulting Group's Knowledge Management Practice, and he is a member of the IBM Institute for Knowledge Management. He has previously consulted in the areas of process reengineering, product development, organization strategy, and design and change management. Yet he focuses on the area of knowledge management, developing strategies for the implementation of KM. He has been with IBM for three years.

Prior to joining IBM, he was a member of Mercer Consulting Group and Andersen Consulting.

Eric has published extensively on knowledge management themes. His articles have appeared in the *Journal of Business Strategy, IABC Communication World*, The *Marsh and McClellan Companies Quarterly, Knowledge Management Yearbook*, and *The Quality Yearbook*.

Eric is a summa cum laude graduate from Brandeis University in economics. He received his M.B.A. with honors from Emory University and has also studied at the London School of Economics and Political Science. He is a member of Phi Beta Kappa and Beta Gamma Sigma. You can reach him at: elesser@us.ibm.com.

Scott H. Oldach is Vice President of Strategic Initiatives for IBM's operations in Europe, and he is headquartered in Paris, France. Prior to accepting this assignment, he was the Vice President of Transformation Consulting Services, responsible for developing the IBM Consulting Group's competency strategy and creating a broad range of consulting methodologies. He is also one of the creators of the IBM Consulting Group. His specialties include process and organizational design, development of information technology strategies and business architectures, and restructuring business resources. He brings a broad industry background to this book, with experience working in airline operations, banking, insurance, consumer packaged goods, petroleum, telecommunications, and agribusiness.

Prior to joining IBM in 1992, Scott worked with Arthur Andersen & Co., Booz, Allen & Hamilton, and the MAC Group. He is the author of a number of articles on corporate change, I/T strategy, and competencies. He is currently writing a book on competing through competencies.

Scott is a graduate of the Massachusetts Institute of Technology with a B.S. in Management Sciences and Operations Research. You can reach him at: oldach@fr.ibm.com.

Laurence Prusak is the Executive Director of the IBM Institute for Knowledge Management, and he also serves as a Managing Principal with IBM Global Services. He has extensive consulting experience, within the U.S. and internationally, in helping firms leverage and optimize their information and knowledge resources. He has been with IBM for three years. Prior to joining IBM Global Services, he was a Principal in Ernst & Young's Center for Business Innovation, specializing in issues of corporate knowledge management.

A respected authority in the field, Larry has lectured and published widely. He is the co-author, with James McGee, of *Managing Information Strategically* (John Wiley & Sons, 1994), and he has co-authored two books with Tom Davenport: *Information Ecology* (Oxford University Press, 1997) and *Working Knowledge* (Harvard Business School Press, 1997). He also edited an anthology of articles on knowledge management, *Knowledge in Organizations* (Butterworth-Heinemann, 1997). His articles have appeared in *Sloan Management Review*, *California Management Review*, and the *International Journal of Information Management*. He has been widely quoted in such publications as *Fortune*, *Business Week*, *CIO*, and *The Economist*.

Larry holds a B.A. in history from Long Island University, an M.A. in economic and social history from New York University (where he completed all of the examinations and course work toward a Ph.D.), and an M.S. in information science from Simmons College. He has guest lectured at Harvard University, the University of California, and New York University. You can reach him at: lprusak@us.ibm.com.

Harvey L. Thompson is a Principal in IBM Global Services, with worldwide responsibility for management consulting on customer-focused client business improvement and reengineering. As corporate program director, he led development and deployment of IBM's business process management techniques and the development of Customer Value Management (CVM). The majority of his consulting work is concentrated on implementation of CVM with clients in a dozen industries around the world.

Harvey is a frequent speaker on the subject of CVM, participating in conferences around the globe. He has also published articles on the subject of CVM, which have appeared in the *Journal of Business Strategy* and other business journals. He is currently completing a book on CVM, soon to be published by McGraw-Hill.

Harvey holds a B.A. in management from North Texas State University and has taken classes at the Wharton School, Arizona State University, and the University of Texas. You can reach him at: hthomp@us.ibm.com.

William A. Tulski, Jr. is a Senior Engineer and the Manager of the Business Systems Modeling Department at the IBM T.J. Watson Research Laboratory. He leads a team responsible for the development of business process modeling tools. He has extensive experience applying computer-based models to solve business problems across many industries.

Bill's research initiatives have been in such areas as product life cycles, product substitution dynamics, the analysis and characterization of competitive markets, and buyer preference characteristics. He has also held marketing and sales positions at IBM and at Litton Systems. He has published articles on business modeling techniques.

Bill holds a BSEE from Drexel University and the ExMSE from the University of Pennsylvania. He was also the Moore Fellow in the Management of Technology at the University of Pennsylvania. You can reach him at: wtulski/watson/ibm@us.ibm.com.

Edward Wakin, Professor of Communications at Fordham University, writes on a variety of business topics, ranging from knowledge management to entrepreneurship. His column for *Beyond Computing*, "Professional Edge," was awarded first place in its category in 1998 by the American Society of Business Press Editors. He has authored scores of articles and authored or co-authored more than 20 books.

Edward has extensive experience handling special editorial assignments for corporations, from annual reports to position papers, and he is nationally known for his corporate communications and editorial workshops. An experienced journalist and editor with such publications as the *New York World-Telegram* and *The Wall Street Journal*, he is also a past winner of the George Polk Award for "distinguished achievement in journalism."

A graduate of Fordham University, Edward has an M.A. in journalism from Northwestern University, an M.A. in sociology from Columbia University, and a Ph.D. in sociology from Fordham University.

Part One

CONFRONTING CHANGE

1

The Challenge of Change, the Response of Transformation

In times of crisis or high turbulence people expect,
indeed demand, great change.
—Joel Barker

Profound changes are affecting all organizations. These changes
challenge organizations to respond by transforming themselves.
A blueprint for transformation—the focus of this book—is sum-
marized in this chapter, which concludes with a road map to the
chapters that follow.

A historical flashback identifies our exploration of change and organizational transformation. The year is 1801, when the visionary Thomas Jefferson became the third president of a nation of awesome potential on a continent with vast, unexplored territory. In the face of the unknown, expeditions were planned, organized, and launched to identify what was out there, all the way to the Pacific Ocean. Before Jefferson sent Merriwether Lewis and George Rogers Clark on their epic 1804-1806 continental exploration, a Lieutenant John Armstrong was one of those who tried and failed to explore the American West. His footnote in United States history is his admission of failure: "This is a business much easier planned than executed."[1]

The lead writer of this chapter is James W. Cortada.

Flashing forward to the mid-1990s, managers echo the lieutenant's frustration as they explore ways and means of transforming their organizations to deal with the unknown in the form of cascading changes. They've been hard at work. An *Economist* study from the mid-1990s showed that over 70 percent of the global companies had launched various types of transformation initiatives, mostly reengineering, during the late 1980s or early 1990s. They concentrated on building effective business processes aligned with more competitive business visions under the banner of becoming more customer-focused, global, and responsive.[2]

Managers have also discovered how difficult a job transformation is. Despite the wide variety of tools available, every published survey that we have seen, including IBM's own internal studies, confirms what most managers already know: transformation is "much easier planned than executed." *CFO* magazine in 1995 was one of the earliest to flag the problem of dissatisfaction with transformation, noting that executives were running into too many unanticipated problems. In 1995 *Information Week* queried U.S. and European executives on reengineering and reported the first major finding that reengineering was not going as well as promised. A 1995 survey of U.S. gas utilities showed that 66 percent had initiated some form of transformation, but only 25 percent of them were satisfied with the results at that point.

Key Findings of U.S. Gas Utilities Survey, 1995

- Percentage of firms that had initiated some form of transformation: **66%**
  (Three reasons for change were reactive: stockholder demands, regulators, some leadership. Most change was related to budget cutting, process reengineering, or reorganizations.)
- Percentage of firms that were satisfied with their transformations so far: **25%**
  (Top three problems faced by management: capital formation, improving efficiencies, and leadership.)

Source: IBM/Southern Gas Association Survey, June 1995

A mid-1990s IBM survey of some 600 managers on their level of satisfaction with transformation confirmed that after a decade of working on transformation, managers were still frustrated (see box). Forty-five percent were not sure they were getting positive results. Sixty percent were only partially satisfied with the outcomes. The responses of managers in this survey sounded like Lieutenant Armstrong revisited. In his case, never having made it even to the west bank of the Missis-sippi, he gave up and turned in his expense account "for himself & Servant, totaling one hundred and ten dollars and thirty-nine ninetieths of a Dollar."[3]

IBM Transformation Survey Results, 1995-1997

- 35% were less than one year into a substantial transformation
  - –Focus was on cost containment, back-room processes, and efficiencies
- 65% were three or more years into a substantial transformation, 35% less than three years into major change
  - –Focus was on investments for market growth, order fulfillment, and supply-chain processes
- 60% were only partially satisfied with their success
- 45% were not sure if they were getting positive results
- 95% said culture was their biggest obstacle
- 80% said leadership was also a major block to transformation
- 25% said I/T was an obstacle to change
  - –Key success factors: commitment and leadership

Key processes being reengineered by 1997:
- Customer service
- Finance and accounting
- Human resources
- Manufacturing processes
- Information technology

Source: 600 managers from corporations and public sector agencies, surveyed between 1995 and 1997, IBM Consulting Group

The Unavoidable Stakes

Managers at the beginning of the 21st century also face the unknown, but without the option of being able to turn back. Company survival is at stake. They have to deal with the question all managers are asking: "How can my company thrive in this period of change?" There's no disagreement on the change part. It's everywhere: in the values and interests of society; in the way children are being raised and educated; in the technologies reshaping school, work, and home; in the way families are organized and businesses structured; in what is happening to entire societies and national economies.

In the current period and for the foreseeable future, *change* has become a source of uncertainty that would unnerve even the founders of the radically new United States. For management, the central issue is how to understand and take advantage of change. The stakes are already evident as some firms thrive and others go out of business almost overnight. Companies come and go, established companies disaggregate, new ones emerge. Entertainment and the Internet, telecommunications and information processing, finance and insurance—all are examples of industries changing and merging in a time of both high risk and high reward.

This book addresses the single overriding concern of executive management: survival and success of their organizations in the face of profound change. All organizations face the same challenge of change, whether they are for-profit companies or nonprofit entities in governmental, charitable, research, or educational arenas. They must respond to the times in which they operate, recognize and confront the conditions they face, and harness their financial, material, and human resources to achieve results. And they must do so in the real (and uncertain) world.

Our basic premise is that all organizations are now in, or are about to enter, a long period of rapid, intense, and continuous change as the economies of the world become one; as the industrial capitalism of the Second Industrial Revolution evolves rapidly into a service-centric, information-based economy; and as a half-century of computer technology finally begins to reshape the very nature of commerce and corporate governance.[4]

The starting point for transformation is planning—planning that is informed, flexible, responsive, and cognizant of what others have done and learned. Then comes the test of execution. The strategies we will discuss and lay out have emerged from the fires of application. They have been put to the test and refined by reality. We present them as practical road maps to managers on their journey to the next economic revolution, a period that economists predict will be different, exciting, and potentially the most rewarding economically in the history of the world.[5]

In response to the challenge of change, transformation encompasses what organizations must do and how they must change internally to respond to the external changes surrounding them. It is change *inside* to keep pace with change *outside*. By *transformation* we mean fundamental changes in how an organization operates and competes in order to achieve significant financial and operational results in performance. Transformation is accomplished through the application of a number of techniques to institutionalize organizational and employee behavior to bring about long-term success. This requires that a variety of techniques be used simultaneously: restructuring, downsizing, reengineering, automation, quality management, and change management. Instead of a single solution, look to a customized portfolio of responses.

Accordingly, we have found that successful transformations have these characteristics:

- an orientation toward customer values and a focus on process rather than function,
- visionary goals and clearly articulated targets dictated by strategic imperatives,
- commitment to radical rethinking and reformulation of business operations, and
- the will to succeed.

Most important, the process of transformation is always holistic. It works best when it involves all parts and major activities of an organization and is implemented in a comprehensive and coordinated manner. In the early 1990s, David Kearns, CEO of Xerox when it was in danger of going out of business, captured the essence of why such a profound change was needed and how it felt: "We realize that we are in a race without a finish line. As we improve, so does our competition. Five years ago, we would have found that disheartening. Today, we find it invigorating."[6]

Management and Transformation

Managing organizations, never an easy or predictable task, is more challenging than ever. In responding to change, managers are only human. They feel comfortable with what they know and they can feel intimidated as they try to fathom what's "out there." It's tempting to search for a "silver bullet" as the answer, a temptation to which managers easily (and understandably) succumb. They have embraced reengineering, time-based competition, employee empowerment, rightsizing, concurrent engineering, reduced hierarchies, and information technology in pursuit of competitive advantage. They have gone all out to get closer to the customer, redesigned corporate cultures, and reached for Total Quality Management. Many are making the effort in an unorganized fashion, while the best are synchronizing their efforts. But a single "silver bullet" has yet to be fired.

After a decade of profound change throughout the economies of the industrialized world, it is necessary to ask: How is change itself changing? What is changing? Where are we headed? Like an explorer preparing for a trip, we improve the quality of our planning by learning as much as possible from others who have already made the trip. Of course there is always the unexpected—which the best plans try to anticipate.

The obvious sources of answers about transformation are those people who have already been "out there" trying to deal with change—executives who have been involved in changing their organizations. IBM has been doing just that over the past half-dozen years by surveying groups of executives on their experiences with transformation. These surveys have included for-profit and nonprofit organizations, large and small companies, high-tech and low-tech firms. They have ranged across manufacturing, retail, distribution, insurance, finance, the public sector, secondary and higher education, and the military. Many of the surveys have been conducted as part of a three-year partnership with Clemson

University through a series of conferences on business transformation in which over 50 firms shared their experiences with each other. Other surveys were conducted within IBM's various divisions worldwide and in industries just beginning transformation (e.g., utilities in the United States, insurance around the world).

While acceptance of the need to deal with change varies by industry, all the major studies on corporate renewal have called for management to acknowledge the reality of change and to deal with it. This finding is fundamental. Acceptance of the need to change is the starting point. It came first among highly competitive industries. At the start of the 1990s, for example, IBM executives—buffeted by global economic change and the rapid evolution of technology—recognized the need for change at the same time as did others in similarly situated industries, such as telecommunications and biomedical firms. In contrast, regulated industries, such as electric and gas providers, remained in denial for a longer period of time before embarking on their transformations.

Mapping the Way

Based on management studies, surveys, and firsthand successes in consulting projects, we have identified five key elements in drawing road maps for transformation:

1. *Organizational change itself has been changing.* What managers are changing and how they are making changes have evolved continuously. Most managers began by curbing expenses, often downsizing and usually reducing resources (e.g., employees, inventory, facilities, debt) but not necessarily the work to be done. That put enormous stress on organizations and people, creating pressure for more fundamental change.[7]

By the early 1990s, two paths became prominent: reengineering processes and improving the quality of goods and services. That was a beginning but not a complete solution, as change followed change. Michael Hammer and James Champy became celebrities with their book on reengineering, while prophets of quality, such as W. Edwards Deming and Joseph Juran, won attention all over the world. The Japanese success in applying quality management practices in the 1970s and 1980s became proof positive that fundamental changes could be made and, indeed, had to be implemented.[8] By the end of the 1990s, we knew that organizational change was less about organizations and more about what people knew, how they worked together, and what tools they used.

2. *Technology is driving a great deal of change and therefore must be harnessed to the advantage of the organization.* Although managers routinely speak of technology as if it were synonymous with information technology, the reality is something else. Yes, computers are front and center in the process of change, but technological influences are coming from all over: telecommunications, biology, chemistry, transportation, new tools, miniaturization and electronics, portable electricity, and new composite materials.

These in turn are changing the economics of technology. For example, as computer chips become more dense and are used in greater quantity, their unit costs come down, in turn leading to greater reliance on this technology and its wider use—from diapers to tires. Another byproduct of technology is the speed with which business can be conducted. Orders are placed online in seconds; 24-hour-a-day, seven-day-a-week ordering has become standard. But as we demonstrate in this book, it is exploitation of the functions of technology, not the devices themselves, that is so important today.

3. *The Age of Information has arrived with a vengeance.* Since General Electric's first commercial application in 1950 of a computer to handle accounting and production in a Kentucky appliance factory, computing has become a standard part of organizations of all sizes in all industries.

Today, companies spend between 1.8 percent and 5 percent of their budgets solely on computing. The computer industry has grown from less than several million dollars in the early 1950s to the mammoth information processing industry of 1999, with more than $500 billion just in products and services. Add in the cost of salaries of people using that technology and the total surpasses $1 trillion annually. Rename the Age of Information the Age of Knowledge Management and the 1.8 percent to 5 percent figure jumps to more than 50 percent.

While popular writers began heralding the "Age of Computers" in the 1960s, the spread of computers didn't gain far-reaching momentum until the late 1970s and early 1980s. Some experts did not acknowledge the profound influence of computing until the United States reached a point in the late 1980s when corporations were installing tens of millions of personal computers annually. As became obvious, the use of so many machines did more than physically alter the look and feel of the modern office. It made new applications almost ubiquitous: e-mail, word processing, the use of spreadsheets, and now e-business. Looking ahead—as the information below suggests—the surge in computing shows no signs of lessening. Thus, it is no surprise that IBM's own experience suggests that in industry after industry the action today is digital in meeting the challenge of melding information management and more traditional economic practices into new business behaviors.

Growth in Population of Personal Computers in the U.S. 1981-1994	
1981	344,000 sold in U.S.
1985	3.29 million sold in U.S.
1993	31 million in U.S. households
1994	70 million total U.S. PC population
Source: IDC, U.S. Department of Commerce	

4. *Organizations and their infrastructures are changing in profound ways.* A generation ago, Alvin Toffler predicted dramatic organizational changes in *Future Shock*. A decade ago, Charles Handy showed us how those changes were coming about.[9] And in the early 1990s, scholars and consultants began documenting cases. When organizations began to flatten, as predicted by the experts, e-mail and other forms of electronic data transfer were enablers and middle managers the immediate target. Eventually, it took raw downsizing to bring about significant flattening organization-wide, the equivalent of hitting someone on the side of the head to get his or her attention.

Meanwhile, other developments were at work. For one thing, English became the most widely used business language in the world during the past two decades. For another, air travel for business increased steadily throughout the 1990s, bringing the far-flung corners of organizations closer to each other. Together, technology, transportation, and common language, in addition to the Internet, have facilitated globalization—a major factor in the spread of process reengineering and corporate restructuring as responses to the need to function globally.

The first businesses to go global were manufacturing firms selling products like aircraft, tractors, automobiles, soft drinks, and electronics. A second wave followed in services with finance, banking, insurance, retail, and transportation. The Internet opened up prospects for additional waves of change: virtual companies that have no warehouses or sales offices, only space in a computer. What became new in the late 1990s was not the rhetoric of globalization—that emerged in the 1980s—but rather the formation of companies that required minimal capital, unlike firms in the pre-PC era that had to invest in bricks and mortar if they wanted to open for business.

Besides the deconstruction and reconstruction of industries, which is now well under way, there is the reconfiguration of horizontally organized supply chains. Products begin with customer demands and move through design, production, and distribution along a physical chain, while vast amounts of information move back and forth along a digital chain. If nothing else, the ability to reconstruct distribution chains is bonding different industries together and creating new alliances while killing off some other industries.

5. *As business environments change dramatically, time becomes a critical issue.* Organizations face complexity, market and competitive challenges, innovation, customer expectations, demands for quality and reliability, and cost pressures. Amidst all these forces of change, time becomes a harsh and unforgiving despot—evident in shrinking windows of opportunity, shortened product cycles, abbreviated schedules for implementing prototypes, and the short life of exclusivity. The introduction of Internet-based sources of business has added yet another time-based dimension, as has recognition of the speed with which knowledgeable employees could exploit or create new business opportunities for their firms.

Many case studies (primarily in magazines) have dramatized the successes and failures of organizations in this environment of change. Like flares in the night to guide explorers, individual cases can indicate where to go or not to go, but they lack context. They don't provide a blueprint for identifying practices that work for companies in *general*. They prompt core questions from managements that want to do more than make plans—that want successful *execution*. Thus, the questions:

- Are there patterns that translate into "rules of the road" or, to use a more popular phrase, "best practices"?
- Have we thus far had enough transformations to understand what's working in organizations that are moving successfully into what can be identified as an Economic Revolution, one characterized by extensive use of communications, computing, information, and services?

The answer to both of these questions is an emphatic yes. A sufficient number of rules of the road and processes have emerged for transformation to succeed in any organization—high-tech or low-tech; small, medium, or large; manufacturing or services; local or global. We can now identify what to change in organizations with greater confidence than a decade ago and we can now provide the tools and approaches that transform organizations. We can exploit experiences in linking business strategies to technologies and in applying new processes and solutions that draw on competency- and knowledge-based approaches. All of this leads to our blueprint for successful transformation based on *knowledge, process*, and *technology*—the three major areas in our presentation.

Successful Transformation

IBM management consultants, like colleagues at rival firms, collect observations about their consulting projects in an organized manner to improve the quality of their consulting. They find that clients who are successful at transforming confront the key questions: What are our future market realities? What is our preferred future state and how do we get there? What capabilities will we need to achieve that state? How do we design a comprehensive program for achieving our vision?

In terms of operational changes, these organizations address equally important questions: How can we achieve excellence? How can we exploit our current capabilities? What new market opportunities can we pursue or create with these capabilities? Which opportunities do we want to pursue? What is the impact of these decisions on our future business and organization?

Companies that succeed with transformation deal with both sets of questions at the same time, in addition to implementing programs of continuous improvement and cost control. That is what we mean by a *holistic* approach. Throughout this book we will analyze many success stories—like the examples that follow—and place them in the context of our blueprint for transformation:

- A U.S.-based fast food restaurant chain, driven by its vision of improving profitability, redesigned its restaurants to exploit technology and facilitate growth.
- A successful direct marketer of clothing and accessories, driven by a vision of reorganizing operations to improve customer retention, grew its customer base and established new markets for its business.
- A major bank focused on operational improvements by redesigning its check processing systems to generate sustained competitive advantage.
- A U.S. utility firm engineered an organization-wide transformation that improved competitiveness, drove down costs, and improved customer service.

In each case, a holistic approach that ranged from understanding the business environment to pulling transformation levers was at work. Figure 1-1 illustrates the blueprint that was used. It is central to this book.

In line with the blueprint, a firm must understand the environmental drivers it cannot escape. These consist of two sets of issues: business conditions and the needs and wants of customers. In the relatively stable past, tracking both was tough enough. In the current period, reality is like the proverbial river that flows continuously. Managers never step into the same river twice. Everything keeps moving in rushing waters that are more like rock-filled rapids than a smooth-flowing river.

In this setting, managers face the task of establishing a business strategy and its servant, business models, to answer the questions they must face: Where are we now? Where do we need to be? What

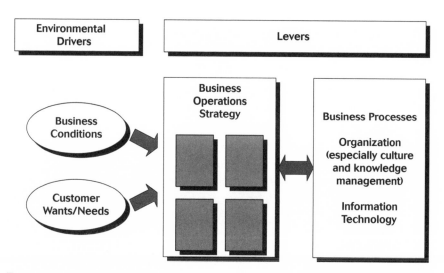

FIGURE 1-1. THE BLUEPRINT FOR TRANSFORMATION USED IN THIS BOOK

capabilities do we need? How do we get there? How do we do this as quickly as possible?

The alignment of business models with overall business strategy must apply across an entire organization, from product innovation[10] to information systems.[11] Different environments call for different business models, with the most effective targeted to specific sets of customers and their needs. Mass customization is deployed to achieve high quality and very individualized products and services. Continuous improvement leads to low-cost, high-quality products, while inventive approaches provide very high differentiation. Mass customization produces a door that fits a newly remodeled home. Mass production turns out a new coffee pot. A detailed bill from a credit card company comes from continuous improvement, while a consultant's recommendations about what a company should do next come from invention. Each serves a purpose.

Armed with business operation strategies, managers can apply a range of tools and techniques to turn goals into reality. Essentially, these tools and techniques are applied across the three fronts we have identified: knowledge, process, and technology. In over two thousand transformation projects, we have found that those that succeeded (the vast majority) involved changes on all three fronts—set within a construct of business strategies. It is the threefold approach that distinguishes this book and separates it from others you have read. It presents a blueprint—complete with examples, scenarios, and tools—for successful transformation.

Environmental drivers and customer-oriented operations strategy are the starting point (Part One of this book). An extensive IBM study of changes in over a half-dozen global industries constitutes a major source of proven techniques for understanding customer needs and wants. We will also cover an often-ignored link: specific ways to tie what customers want to daily decision making in the organization. It is a unique approach that is carefully honed at IBM: customer value management. Add a crucial element that managers want and need: guidelines for identifying workable business strategies in the midst of uncertainty about which approaches will work for them.

The heart of transformation are the three levers that must be pulled to institute changes that succeed and last: knowledge, process, and technology (Parts Two, Three, and Four, respectively, of this book):

- **Knowledge-Based Organizations:** We need to take a new look at organizational changes. Instead of yesterday's focus on such issues as organizational charts and downsizing, we will look at what it means to manage knowledge and to leverage it with competencies. This leads to crucial questions that we will address: What is the knowledge organization? How does it work? Where does it fit in? How are knowledge-based competencies leveraged? We link knowledge management to other aspects of business activity—process management and use of Information Technology (IT)—and move from the theoretical to the nuts and bolts of application.

- **Managing by Process:** While most organizations have tried reengineering, updating is needed on best practices. There have been some startling developments just in the past half-dozen years that managers need to understand and take into account. Once reengineered, most companies want to manage processes, not just organizations, a need that is met by making governance an ongoing task. In the ensuing transformation, process emerges as the decisive "X" factor. After two decades of experience with process management, effective practices have emerged that facil-itate directed change. Understanding these practices is imperative.

- **Leveraging Technology:** As a necessary part of transformation, information technology drives, influences, and shapes organiza-tional change. It not only enables and implements, it also causes changes. After a half-century of commercial computing, best practices are emerging with answers to universal management questions: What technologies should we use? Why? What are the "killer applications"? What's next? What about e-business? These are questions to be addressed and answered within the context of our blueprint for transformation. You may be surprised, in this book written by IBMers, by the limited attention we give to tech-nology. That's because technology, as crucial as it is, constitutes one part of a whole and belongs to a larger process of change and growth.

Finally, knowledge, process, and technology must all come togeth-er in a series of concurrent steps to advance transformation. There are actions to take, pitfalls to avoid—guided and supported by the experi-ences of a large number of organizations worldwide. Amid the uncer-tainty bred by change, enough organizations have successfully explored the territory of transformation to provide maps, landmarks, and guidelines in dealing with the changing rules of the game in an information-driven age of exploration, discovery, and surprises.

Summary

Change is begetting change. For every organization, transformation as a response to change is crucial to long-term prosperity. The good news for managers is that a proven blueprint for transformation is at hand. It establishes a foundation in environmental drivers: business conditions and customer wants/needs. It designates a place for busi-ness operations strategy and integrates the three levers of successful transformation—knowledge, process, and technology.

What is now available will provide managers with the know-how, information, and techniques to deal with change. Managers need all the help they can get, operating as they do in a business environment that calls for continuous charting, fast-paced decisions, and highly responsive strategies. Now they can apply and benefit from what we have learned about transforming organizations in response to the ongoing challenge of change.

The changes in management agendas and in leadership roles are rooted in the way business is changing. The rules of the game are changing as profoundly today as they did with the First Industrial Revolution in the 18th century and the Second in the 19th century. This calls for a searching look at just how the rules are changing and how this affects management at all levels—the focus of the next chapter.

For Further Reading

William J. Baumol, Sue Anne Batey Blackman, and Edward N. Wolff, *Productivity and American Leadership: The Long View* (Cambridge, MA: MIT Press, 1989).

Baumol and his team of economists present a very detailed and sensible analysis of productivity, with comments on the role of technology and corporate restructuring.

Charles Handy, *The Age of Uncertainty* (Boston: Harvard Business School Press, 1989).

This philosopher by training has written a series of books describing a flatter, competency-driven organization of the future. This is the book that launched the popular discussion of this topic.

Richard K. Lester, *The Productive Edge* (New York: W.W. Norton, 1998).

A distinguished economist looks at how five major industries are changing to enhance corporate productivity and growth. The book documents how firms on the brink of disaster routinely come back alive and thrive.

Jorge Reina Schement and Terry Curtis, *Tendencies and Tensions of the Information Age* (New Brunswick, NJ: Transaction Publishers, 1995).

This is the most current discussion available about the evolution of knowledge workers. It also is a useful review of the nature of their work and it has an excellent collection of bibliographic citations.

Don Tapscott, *The Digital Economy: Promise and Peril in the Age of Networked Intelligence* (New York: McGraw-Hill, 1996).

The author, while not an economist, clearly understands the impact of technology on corporations. While he overstates the case for the role of computing, his points clearly are embraced by many executives in high-tech firms.

How the Rules of the Game Are Changing

We are all prisoners of our past. It is hard to think of things except in the way we have always thought of them. But that solves no problems and seldom changes anything.
—Charles Handy

In addressing the dimensions of change and the implications for management, this chapter documents the ways in which business activities are changing, by drawing on extensive studies by IBM and by identifying the lessons learned. What's happening represents the early stage of a new wave of economic transformation of historic proportions.

In the accelerated history of the Information Age, the Barnes & Noble/Amazon.com confrontation became an overnight landmark in the topography of competitive surprises. Barnes & Noble, one of the most successful national retail book chains in North America, operates stores that are a book lover's delight. Store inventories routinely run to more than 110,000 volumes, which are sold at competitive prices. Add special book buys, secondhand volumes, magazines, helpful sales people, music, coffee, and opportunities to browse and you have a comfortable environment where customers feel at

The lead writer of this chapter is James W. Cortada.

home. In sum, a Barnes & Noble bookstore makes book buying a multi-layered experience.

In the past decade, the chain expanded rapidly. Business was brisk, management excellent. Growth was often a function of how many new stores could be opened in more cities. The company was on a roll. Then Amazon.com appeared online, practically overnight, presenting itself as the world's largest bookstore with over two million titles available for sale—a virtual bookstore with no shelves, no salespeople, and no doors to walk through. It created a sensation in the book world with a "store front" that was an address on the Internet—Amazon.com.

Customers could visit the store at any time of day or night, without leaving home. They could browse books by subject, author, or title, get background on books that interested them, order online from a vast electronic catalog at substantial discounts, and count on prompt delivery. For good measure, they could "chat" about books and authors. Within months, Amazon.com became nationally known and a serious challenge to Barnes & Noble.

A struggle developed between old and new ways of doing business. Barnes & Noble, with capital, infrastructure, a good management team, and brand recognition, squared off against an upstart with no stores, a young management team, and a strong Internet presence. Barnes & Noble worried about Amazon's potential to destroy its vast investment in a network of stores, but it also read the signs on the Information Highway. So it expanded its own Internet marketing.

What was Barnes & Noble to do in the face of an Internet challenger? How could Amazon make a profit and fight off the large book chains? How could the problem appear so quickly and with such corporate life-threatening possibilities?

This was not an isolated battle of bookstores. It was yet another demonstration of the changing rules of the game—a game being played in the marketplace, in the stock market, and in the courts, and ultimately decided on the bottom line.

An Internet-based company took on a well-established corporate giant that was riding high. New vs. old, bricks vs. bits, structures vs. silicon, traditional merchandising vs. telemerchandising.

An Economic Revolution

As various economists and historians are acknowledging, we are entering an economic revolution at least as far-reaching, if not more so, than the First (1730s-1820s) and the Second (1870s-1940s) Industrial Revolutions. As in the first two revolutions, widespread conversions to a new business environment are taking place—by choice and out of necessity. This time the accelerating rate of change puts management under relentless pressure to keep up. The more management understands and responds to what's happening, the more successful the organizations will be; the less responsive, the more endangered.

Ideally, managers want a reliable way to forecast the future so that they can blend their strategies into the mainstream of economic opportunities, avoid dead ends, and anticipate, then counter, competition. In attempting to deliver what managers want, the "how-to" literature is vast and speculations about the future fill shelf after shelf in a Barnes & Noble store. But the problem is that no forecast is guaranteed to cover all possibilities, as managers are continually reminded when they come face to face with the startling variety of predictions from economists and futurists.

On the one hand, as physicists point out, reality is chaotic. On the other, companies can't sit still. They must meet the latest customer wants and needs, grow their business, and earn profits. They must make decisions about tomorrow—today. Fortunately, all is not lost for managers. They can adopt an attitude that willingly accepts change as an opportunity. This is a position that's best implemented when informed by a business model or a sense of where the business needs to go. Thus we see the need to develop a mental construct and apply an approach that responds to and even anticipates what's happening in their economic environment. It's an approach that parallels a formulation used by biologists.[1] By thinking in terms of operating in an environment—an economic ecology—managers confront change as opportunity rather than threat. In doing so, they:

- know the geography of their environment,
- understand where they fit in the food chain,
- are able to run quickly toward their next meal or away from a predator,

- change their behavior to exploit changes in climate or the emergence of new food sources, and
- evolve their species as needed.

Management thinking is facilitated by another variation of the biological analogy: systems thinking, an idea that builds on each of these ecological points. Companies are viewed as micro-ecologies, governed by processes that provide stimulus and response, feedback and consequences on all activities, and in which everything affects everything else. The notion has been emerging in business circles since the early 1900s, when Frederick W. Taylor began writing about "scientific management." His arguments included process thinking and systems analysis. By thinking of a department as part of a larger whole, a manager can begin to understand the value of seeing the entire enterprise as part of a larger entity—a national or international economic system. Then the implications for strategy and tactics become clearer.

This is not esoteric thinking. Sociologist Margaret Wheatley, for one, has made an effective case for an ecological approach. If, for example, you think of your firm as operating in a business ecology as a participant and part of an economic environment, partnerships and alliances make a great deal of sense. You can view horizontal and vertical organizational structures as options. Think of the lion in the jungle: it does not need to evolve into a shade tree to get midday shelter; it simply partners with a tree for a few hours. On the other hand, it must have its own ability to run to get food—a core competency based on its physical infrastructure.

By understanding how the new economic environment is beginning to operate, a manager—like the lion in the jungle—can begin to identify what to hunt, what dangers to be aware of, how to live safely, and when to eat, sleep, and work. Thus, in the absence of an infallible crystal ball, we can focus on identifying and understanding existing trends *that are at the forefront of the changes overtaking the business environment.* We can prepare ourselves for change by identifying what the emerging new ecology looks like.

Before exploring that ecology, we propose that instead of thinking of the emerging world as a Third Industrial Revolution, think of it as an *Economic* Revolution, because our findings demonstrate that the changes are far broader than those in the manufacturing sector and that they stretch into the foreseeable future. Some of the changes are one-time, such as the shift to electronic commerce. Others are long-term, such as the emergence of information as the dominant element in both products and services. Nonetheless, these changes cover all aspects of economic and social life and are not bounded by continent or country. Unlike the two Industrial Revolutions, which were largely limited to Europe and the United States and later included parts of East Asia, change is occurring concurrently and rapidly on a global basis across almost every traditional business sector, industry, and company. This is our point of departure—the totality and speed of this change.

The lesson for managers is that they must think of business transformation in far broader and more comprehensive terms than suggested previously by experts on reengineering and corporate cultural transformation or by marketing consultants worried about share, innovation, and branding. Change is happening, to use our ecological analogy, at a rate of speed and on a scale resembling an erupting volcano that destroys millions of acres of surrounding land, a tidal wave that overwhelms a shoreline, or a forest fire that devastates plant and animal life. A broad process of regeneration of the environment is at work. Given what we see and what economists are beginning to document, these analogies are not exaggerations.

As with far-reaching natural change, new opportunities emerge—at the expense of those who cannot escape the impact of change. In the aftermath of natural disasters, new plants and trees grow, and animals reappear. In the aftermath of economic changes, organizations that respond to new opportunities emerge stronger than ever and new organizations that capitalize upon opportunity come to the fore. It is already happening and we can safely predict much more to come. The organizations that succeed are the ones that understand and respond to the magnitude of the economic revolution that is already under way.

Identifying and Understanding Change

IBM's response to the challenge of change is instructive. Some years ago, the company began studying the changing economy of the world within the framework of marketing in order to sell its products and services in over 140 countries. But that soon proved too narrow a focus. Just as does every company, IBM needed to deal with the changing economy globally and to advise its customers across the full range of business activities and planning. It became obvious that IBM's "marketing studies" had to be expanded in scope, range, and coverage.

IBM's customers expected nothing less. They recognized the growing role of electronics and computing in this new ecology and expected companies in networking, computing, and telecommunications to show the way. In response, IBM consultants began a global study, code-named Watershed, to understand, industry by industry, country by country, what was changing, the trigger events that were causing change, and how management should respond.[2]

It became clear—after examining more than a half-dozen industries—that the most obvious driver of change and the one that all firms must take into account is the emerging digital marketplace. Changes are occurring at four levels: processing, enterprises, industries, and boundaries of industries. The greatest changes are emerging at the inter-industry level, where executives in many industries are reporting that they face the most dramatic and also the most problematic changes. The good news is that new business opportunities also are appearing, often resulting from the ability to share customer and supplier information across industries. We already are seeing this development in the mass media, office applications, content providers, telecommunications, distribution, education, entertainment, computer sales, and consumer electronics. And this is only the beginning.

As IBM's studies confirm, fundamental changes are well under way in the historic shift from an industrial to a digital economy. (The box on pages 26-27 catalogs the multiple themes at work.) Not only can everything that was identified as cutting-edge be implemented today with current technology and expertise, it is being implemented and cost-justified by one firm after another. The boundary between cutting-edge and standard practice is disappearing. Tomorrow is becoming hard to separate from today.

Watershed has documented three trends in the forefront of what is happening in business. These trends dramatize the ways in which the rules are changing:

Multiple Themes at Work

- Design, build, sell, and buy anywhere, anytime
- Time- and location-independent work and play
- Free or unlimited consumer choice
- Free for all—no or very low entry or exit barriers
- Globally optimized resources (predictive, sense and respond, customer-supplier linked)
- Global knowledge accessibility
- Value networks (seamless, dynamic, focused competencies, dis-intermediation, and assembly of new value coalitions)
- Increasing consumer power and move to presumption (vs. consumption), i.e., the consumer will order and schedule production and delivery of offering
- Electronic and physical channels will co-exist for a while.
- Consumers will use multiple channels—physical to digital—in all aspects of their lives.
- Customer segmentation will occur in three tiers (all of which will be used simultaneously).
  First by Moment of Value of Event
  Second by Disposable Income
  Third by technology astuteness of the user
- Firms will become more customer-intimate and will be more precise in targeting consumers
- Though individuals will have network access, the degree of exploitation of interconnectivity will be higher between business and business than between business and consumer in the near term.
- Firms will shift to Customer Life Share capture rather than Individual Transaction profitability.
- Owning the content is no guarantee of winning the future. Owning the context (or access of navigation point) will provide most leverage.

- Government intervention will occur on strategic issues, though it may not be successful.
- While disintermediation will occur in many areas (direct enablement), reintermediation will occur in others (where collaboration increases group power).
- While business reach or brands may be more global, production and customer reach will be more through multi-local approaches.
- Consumer preferences and adoption rates are ethnocentric despite ubiquitous channel access.
- Different regions of the world may end up at different points.
- Unusual global exchanges will form, e.g., risk securization and exchange.

- *First,* business-to-consumer marketing will rely less and less on a single business model in relationships with customers. Instead, it will leverage multiple avenues of contact for each customer and will focus on capturing each "moment of value" as it arises. This trend builds on the significant experiences already gained in company-to-company relations through both electronic data interchange (EDI) and other forms of electronic communications and traditional marketing practices.

- *Second,* "stealth companies" will appear with virtual organizational structures and completely different cost and performance dynamics to severely challenge established companies. The pressure will be on to mount a competitive response, as presaged by the Barnes & Noble/Amazon.com confrontation.

- *Third,* the basis of competition will move from cost and value to imagination, with success determined by the speed with which new creative ideas are generated, synthesized, and implemented. Core competencies will revolve around creativity, entrepreneurial zeal, and institutional dynamism.

Watershed found that managers already are confronting these three changes as they evolve from traditional approaches of running businesses. (Figure 2-1 graphically captures the historical evolution of

Attribute	Pre-Industrial Era	Industrial Era	Post-Industrial Era	Electronic Era
Volume Type	Few One-at-a-time	Many All-of-a-kind	Large Engineered variety	Modular design Infinite variety
Approach / Channel	Job shop (Make to order) Few	Mass Production (Build to buy/sell) Firm-controlled	Flexible Mfg. (Build to order) Many channels	Modular Design (Predictive Mfg.) Customer-defined
Cycle Time	Long (years)	Short (months)	Very short (weeks)	Immediate
Firm Orientation	Physical/Physical	Customer Delight	Customer Responsive	Empowered Customer
Product/ Workspace	Customer Satisfaction	Physical/Partly Electronic	Physical/ Electronic	Electronic/ Electronic
Value Chains	Disconnected and small	Physical/Partly Electronic	Interconnected across Firms	Virtual and global
Company Role	Order Taker	Integrator	Optimizer	Demand Responder

FIGURE 2-1. THE HISTORICAL EVOLUTION OF BUSINESS PRACTICES

business practices.) Most of what is described in the media, in books and articles, at seminars, or through consulting projects concerns activities that can now be characterized as "Post-Industrial Era." However, IBM found that a growing number of its customers for computers, networking, and services are well into the "Electronic Era." While the characteristics of the era are becoming increasingly self-evident, the ways in which they are put into action are not so clear and automatic and thus cannot be taken for granted.

How Change Is Changing

Studying changes in business alone was not enough. In a separate but related study conducted by IBM consultants from 1996 to 1998, research was broadened to explore social, economic, and political trends (see box on page 29). Experts in these areas joined technologists and scientists at the Watson Research Laboratories and the IBM Consulting Group to document what was happening. Together, they agreed that the emerging features of the new eco-environment—in work, commerce, industry structures, and technology—were changing more rapidly and dramatically than companies at large were taking

Major Trends

1. Relatively low or stable inflation with increasing employment opportunities

2. Dominant government fiscal policies moving toward fiscal restraint/deficit reduction

3. Economic growth greatest in Asia and its industrial consumer population

4. Tension between religious fundamentalism and modern economic/political forces

5. Minor wars and environmental degradation but no catastrophic global war or environmental crisis

6. Aging population in industrialized countries

7. Increased proportion of women in marketplace and in senior positions

8. Increasing employee ownership and profit sharing in firms

9. Increased competition from smaller, leaner organizations

10. Continued creation of a global middle-class lifestyle, fueled by travel, tourism, immigration, global companies, and brands

into account. Talking about change is not the same as grasping its full dimensions and fast pace, not to speak of keeping up with it.

Technology is changing the nature of work itself—what people actually do to earn a living, the tasks they perform, the way they allocate time, how and why they do what they do. Change is as close as a PC monitor, where the amount of time and effort interacting with computer-based systems continually increases in quantity and importance. This in turn requires greater technical skill and aptitude. Even tools used in traditionally low-tech jobs have become technologically sophisticated. Consider a worker in the utility industry repairing a gas leak. Where he once dug a ditch to locate a broken pipe, today he uses sensing devices coupled with small drilling units to pinpoint a leak, which is then plugged with new composite materials. It's not necessary even to look that far to grasp the digital dominance in everyday living.

The nature of commerce is also changing, as illustrated by the Amazon.com example, among so many. Ordering by phone has become commonplace, joined by the PC, the Internet, and Web-enabled television in almost one-third of all homes in most of the industrialized parts of the world. Companies and industries are changing continuously, their boundaries blurred and breached by digital invaders. Industries emerge that have no names, last a few years, and then evolve into other forms.[3] Then there are the universal changes in technology, as computers appear in all sizes and shapes—and not just as computers (e.g., toys, smart cars, and toasters). All of this takes place in a telecommunications infrastructure that can deliver substantial amounts of data to individuals, homes, and businesses, creating an age of information overload.

Growth in information is not new news. Growth in the availability of information is. From a business perspective, four specific developments have had a direct impact on the bottom line of every corporation:

• consumer access to legal and consumerism-related data and services,
• quick availability of information via the Internet,
• low cost of information (most in computer files), and
• tools to find information and access it immediately.

These four features constitute an "information revolution" by making it possible for a consumer to have at least as much data as a vendor (or perhaps even more), thereby shifting the marketplace balance of power from the supplier to the customer. This overturns the information advantage of suppliers.

The historical context of what is happening illuminates its significance. In identifying waves of change, historians point out that we are going through a tidal wave in growing standards of health, lifestyles, and economic well-being. They present accumulating evidence that dissemination of new technologies and information, along with expanding political alternatives, is creating new opportunities for companies and people—opportunities to accumulate wealth and possessions and to develop individual freedom to create new lifestyles that are varied and highly individualized.[4]

Trend: Product Proliferation

Proliferation of products is growing through the ability of manufacturers to build custom-made products—the idea of mass customization—such as automobiles, blue jeans, and furniture. More standard products are also available, such as personal computers from over 150 vendors.

Was it easier for a customer to buy when he or she had only three or four standard options? Does a customer really want over one hundred options? How do you know as a vendor if you are competitive? These are questions being asked today.

Implications for management:

- Pricing becomes more complex and dynamic as a product, business, or industry becomes disaggregated or differentiated.
- Branding becomes more important as customers seek out trust, relationships, and quality.
- Global visibility is crucial for products, services, and pricing, which gives consumers potential to build their own pricing and value propositions.

Differentiating a product anybody can make by adding services and information becomes important.

These trends suggest that companies and industries must create new and varied value propositions. What models, if any, exist in already-established industries that you can apply in your business? What changes in processes and in the way we deal with the eco-environment will allow your firm to move down the experience curve faster toward the new economy?

Waves of change continue to make an impact on the environment, prices, and demographics. Problems come in the wake of these changes: pollution (particularly in poor countries); continuing disruptions by such natural catastrophes as fires, earthquakes, and volcanic eruptions; and electrical power interruptions caused by violent weather and floods in overbuilt areas. Wars between nations and among people continue to take a toll, as does crime in the streets. For their part, demographers cite the population growth that is projected to expand globally through the first half of the next century, with the greatest growth coming in the poorest and least-industrialized sectors of the world.[5]

Values are a powerful driving force in the changes that are under way. All through this century, the wholesale migration of families from farms and villages to ever-growing urban centers has diluted strong family and cultural bonds and revolutionized values. In 1900, approximately 80 percent of the world's population lived in small villages or on farms. By 1950, that same percentage lived in cities, an extraordinary shift.[6] In Europe, since World War II, internal migrations to cities often involved over one-third of a nation's population, raising new issues about women's rights, child-rearing practices and responsibilities, the roles of church and school, political options, and individual rights, not to mention issues related to privacy. The mother on the farm who raised her children with the help of relatives now works in an office, factory, or law firm and must rely on day care and schools to help rear her children (with the father playing an increasingly important domestic role). The male farmer now is more likely to be an urban office worker or a traveling sales representative.

No part of the world is escaping the impact of change. Its global influences reach into the nooks and crannies of national life. Belgian officials worry about the effect of American movies on local values. The French government passes laws to slow the incursion of English into the French language. East Europeans, with influences from television, shed authoritarian rule in favor of democracy. The sale of birth control pills in Latin America surges, despite urgings of the Catholic Church. Asian students flock to U.S. colleges and universities to acquire American "know-how" and in the process adopt new values and attitudes that they then bring home. Japan builds million-dollar golf courses and cheers for American baseball. National celebrities become instant global personalities, whether in sports (Michael Jordan) or business (Bill Gates). The Internet makes it possible to talk to anyone, anywhere, anytime.

The global convergence of all manner of telecommunications into a massive global infrastructure is a backbone of the new economic order. As an indication of its magnitude, in 1995 126 companies in the U.S. alone were involved in mergers in telecommunications, with a

Trend: Decline in Physical Markets

For centuries people bought and sold products and services in physical markets, from bazaars to shopping centers—from a predetermined spot. Goods were brought to a store and customers took them away. But now there is a growing trend toward disembowelment of physical markets, with eye-to-eye, face-to-face selling and buying increasingly giving way to e-commerce—doing business over the telephone, by television, or on the Internet.

Implications for management:
- Customer expectations of the physical decor, product, and price always existed, but with electronic commerce that goes away. What replaces it? Do we treat product pricing on the Internet the same as we do pricing at a garage sale or a fancy department store?
- Standards for performance and service also change. How do you get support for a product that is broken or that a customer wants to return?
- Gone would be the physical touch and feel that customers are used to in looking at a product. How do you exploit freshness in foods if you sell them remotely? How do we ensure the safety of a product? Which nation's regulations apply?
- Delivery economics change when a product is sold out of a store versus directly from a factory or a warehouse. To what extent will a customer pay for delivery in a virtual market?
- Loss of a merchant, loss of loyalty to a brand: Are these precursors to a universal commodity market?
- Market definitions change, as do identities of industries and suppliers.

The loss of physical markets already is demonstrating the ability of new entrants to come into traditional markets without investing heavily in capital expenditures. This becomes the age of the broker who surfs electronic markets to give customers the "best deal," providing intermediary, agent-like services. Customers get into the open bidding game for mortgages, low-cost capital, and tailored services.

total value of $39.1 billion.[7] IBM's survey of intended expenditures on telecommunications globally led to the finding that the percentage spent on telecommunications will rise from 3.7 percent (in 1996) to more than 4.5 percent by the turn of the century.[8] The percentages are not so crucial as the rate of growth in expenditures—an uptick of almost one-third—which points to enormous transformation.

By looking at changes on an industry-by-industry basis and then examining broader sociological and economic trends, we confirm the inescapable conclusion that a period of tumultuous change is under way. The pattern of change affects companies differently, varies by industry, and alternates and fluctuates, but there's no mistaking the overall direction. It's tempting to underestimate change in industries that seem relatively unchanged or to overestimate change in fast-paced industries. But that does not count in the big picture. We are experiencing historic changes across the board, affecting finance and business, social conditions, technology, and values. As scientists have maintained for over a half-century, life and activity are processes, operating with feedback mechanisms and continuous change in the environment. Success depends on understanding that environment, adjusting to it, seizing the opportunities at hand, and acting upon them—like the lion who must size up his environment so that he can find his food.

The New Competition

Companies don't need to wait for a consensus on how to deal with the changing environment. Nor can they do so in the face of the unprecedented risk of being left behind. They can and must identify the patterns and trends that are emerging and then apply workable (open-ended) answers. See how capital races around the world for both companies and consumers. It is commoditized as it travels with ease and variety, oblivious of geography and national borders. Thus, it is no accident that interest rates at the end of the 1990s hit the lowest level in over four decades. Demand drives capital around the world in seconds. Individuals are accessing it every time they use a credit card or draw on a line of credit as the number of credit cards available grew exponentially between 1980 and 1990. Banks move capital around the world electronically, impervious to controls by central banks. Everyone can get the "best rate" for capital, often finding it regardless of personal credit history. The amount of information available to a manager on capital, money, and credit is nothing less than spectacular.[9]

Information is flowing even more freely than capital. It can be gathered on just about any subject by anybody, leading to highly informed competitors and consumers. Recent studies on patents and copyrights point to their declining importance when technology, products, and industries are changing rapidly. They simply do not serve— as they once did—as barriers to entry or as protection of assets.[10]

A more subtle development has been the homogenization of business, intellectual, and government professionals around the world. They all speak the same language of bits and bytes, killer applications, and networking. Their jobs are the same in form and in substance. In addition to the likelihood that they speak English, a manager in Germany has no trouble discussing business problems with a counterpart in Hong Kong; an executive from Chicago easily compares notes with a customer in Calcutta. For their part, customers are demanding the same level of quality and variety from one nation to another, especially from a vendor who sells a product in multiple countries. Professionals even are dressing alike and sharing common interests in sports, entertainment, and lifestyles. (To take into full account the rising power of the customer, Chapter 3 will focus on how to benefit from the trend.)

From a management perspective, if form follows function, then the implications are obvious. Not only large companies but businesses of all sizes are restructuring to compete on a wider and wider scale. They are reengineering and redesigning processes and corporate structures to achieve global reach and to deliver goods and services in a timely manner. The downsizing of companies in the industrialized West in the late 1980s and throughout the 1990s, which cost millions of jobs (1.8 million in the U.S. alone), created millions of new jobs in the late 1990s (estimated at 10 million in the U.S.)—but with a significant difference. There are proportionately fewer middle managers, but more technically skilled users of information technology. Instead of small satellite offices, there are mobile offices, "virtual staffs," alliances, partnerships, and project staffers. It's no longer clear and simple who works for whom, when, and for how long.

Inevitably, the way companies do business is changing at a rate that defies conventional projections. As a company, IBM illustrates the point. In about 1980, approximately 90 percent of the company's business came from sales of hardware; ten years later, that figure was just over 50 percent. In the late 1990s, it was less than half.[11]

All companies are caught up in the global phenomenon of the Internet, which in its first twenty years was accessed only by U.S. government officials, academics, and a limited number of defense workers. Since the Internet exploded—unpredictably—in the early 1990s, anybody in the world with a modem-equipped personal computer and a telephone line has the world at his or her doorstep. While estimates of the number of users are unreliable, the Internet boom nonetheless is staggering. In 1994, several million had potential access. In 1996, that number climbed to over 15 million in the U.S. alone and in 1998 it had risen to at least 70 million globally.[12]

What Does It All Mean?

Given the scope and speed of change, what are the key implications for management? At IBM, our primary and secondary research and our surveys are already providing answers that support and expand upon our firsthand consulting experiences. It is now possible to make educated calculations, pursue solutions, and plan effectively. It is also necessary to act or risk being left behind.

What stands out is the rise of specificity among products and services offered to customers. Every major industry is experiencing the pressure to provide a more varied set of offerings. Increasingly, companies are finding that they must create products and services highly tailored to ever-increasing numbers of customers. Groups of customers are forming to protest or support an issue or a product. When their interest disappears, as is happening faster—regardless of whether the focus is a product, service, fad, or political issue—they reform later into new individual or group customer demands. Nothing drives this development more than the Internet, which remains a challenge in search of many different and varied paths to profit. Despite the enormous amount of publicity and attention the Internet has received, many companies still are figuring out how to make a profit by using it. So the hunt is on for profitable business models for operating in the new Internet environment.

Time has become an elusive variable, with the one certain prediction that this time revolutionary change is running at high speed. The First Industrial Revolution (1730s-1820s) took over a half-century to show its hand and nearly a full century to play out. The Second Industrial Revolution (1870s-1940s) took about three decades to make a dramatic impact on the economic landscape and just slightly less than a half-century to fully deploy. In both cases the driving issues were scale (how much one needed to make a profit), deployment (how much and how long to get new processes and technologies into place), and acceptance (overcoming resistance).

The First and Second Industrial Revolutions were fueled by energy, people, and capital, eventually blending into the right mix to function effectively. We clearly are going through the same process, with such gating factors as access to the right skills in sufficient quantity, the right amount of capital and technology, and the right size of markets to make a profit. Recent experience indicates that the emerging economic revolution will take far less time than the first two, at least one-third less time than the last one in making a dramatic impact.

To put the outlook in historical perspective, the current global transformation will have the same economic and social impact as the move from cottage industries to factories (1700s) and from small enterprises to corporations (1800s/early 1900s). Given the fact that the new era has been emerging since the 1980s at an accelerated pace, it is our expectation that management has less than one decade remaining to complete a significant portion of its transformation. Anything less than a sense of urgency places any organization at serious risk.

So much for sounding the alarm. On the positive side, the environment is filled with unprecedented opportunities for existing companies of all sizes and for new companies yet to emerge.

Summary

The realities leave no choice: face up to them or be swept away by change. Management must deal with the positive and negative realities of the environment, capitalize on opportunities, and respond to threats from competitors. The main factors are clear: global commerce, the rapid development of technologies, the volatility of the marketplace, the rise of new structures, and the continuous stream of new competitors.

Success always begins by understanding the environment, which is why business managers continually monitor what's happening. That explains the high esteem of a business thinker like Peter F. Drucker, who weaves history and past experience with deep insight into current realities. It is why experts using such compelling terms as "ecologies" and "ecosystems" command attention. And it explains the widespread focus in the past two decades on customer needs and wants.

To confront the business environment and to operate effectively, companies must (as already emphasized) integrate knowledge-based organization, process, and technology. All three must be brought to bear in a structured manner as an integrated whole, as a system whereby an organization creates an architecture or blueprint for doing business. Success depends on the combination of all components interacting and meshing. They must all come together.

The emerging paradigm is being defined and applied by practitioners, not theorists or academics. This means that managers and professional staffers, working with consultants, are transforming businesses one by one. The challenge is to transform quickly and comprehensively while continuing to conduct profitable businesses. The mission of this book is to show how to do it, beginning with the judge and jury who define and determine business success: customers—the greatest number, the wealthiest, and the most informed in the history of the world, and thus the focus of the next chapter.

For Further Reading

James W. Cortada, *The Rise of the Knowledge Worker* (Boston: Butter-worth-Heinemann, 1998).

This is a collection of papers and chapters written by a wide variety of economists, historians, and sociologists over the years about the growing proportion of office workers in the U.S. economy.

John L. Daniels and N. Caroline Daniels, *Global Vision: Building New Models for the Corporation of the Future* (New York: McGraw-Hill, 1993).

Drawing on much of the work done by IBM in helping clients operate global businesses, this book describes the various ways this is being done, from strategy to tactics.

Jeremy Rifkin, *The End of Work: The Decline of the Global Labor Force and the Dawn of the Post-Market Era* (New York: G.P. Putnam's Sons, 1995).

Although the author is relatively negative about the consequences of technology on the future of work, he provides a great deal of new material on the general subject. The book was widely read when it first came out.

Don Tapscott, *The Digital Economy: Promise and Peril in the Age of Networked Intelligence* (New York: McGraw-Hill, 1996).

This was one of the first of the new wave of books to appear in the second half of the 1990s that began to reflect the changes growing out of the post-reengineering and post-downsizing activities of the late 1980s and early 1990s. It is well informed and clearly written.

3

Making Customers into Partners

To satisfy the customer is the mission and
purpose of every business.
—Peter Drucker

*This chapter describes Customer Value Management (CVM), a
set of approaches for building customer loyalty and attracting
greater market share by making customer-dictated needs and
wants an integral part of business design. We will describe what
CVM is and how to implement and sustain it. We will also articulate its benefits.*

When a utility company and a financial services firm
went all-out to address the issue of customer satisfaction, they started from opposite directions to
answer the critical twofold question: *Where do our
customers want us to be and how do we get there?*

The utility company started with a menu of "customer needs"
that were internally developed by its management as targets for quality improvement. Power outages in an area regularly battered by
strong winds and rain were high on the list, an obvious place to drive
improvement as part of a firm-wide effort to win the prestigious
Deming Quality Award.

The lead writer of this chapter is Harvey L. Thompson.

Management proceeded to reduce the length of outages. Downtime between power failure and return to power was reduced from several minutes to just a few seconds per event. Management celebrated its success and went on to other internally defined objectives. In due course, the firm won the Deming award. And the CEO, who drove the quality effort, subsequently retired with his laurels.

No sooner had his successor taken over than he confronted a paradox. He was head of a firm with a national reputation for quality, winner of the Deming award, and a success in meeting *what management had defined* as customer needs and wants, particularly in reducing the average amount of time per outage. Hadn't management delivered what customers wanted? The answer from customers, as relayed by the public regulatory agency, was **NO!** Being customer-*sensitive* was not enough. The firm had to be customer-*aware*.

As it turned out, a major source of customer dissatisfaction was not how long the outages lasted so much as how many there were in the first place. Regardless of length, customers still had to reset every bedside alarm, every stovetop timer, every VCR digital display, and every time-bound electrical device in the house. So they were complaining to the regulatory agency, notwithstanding management's metrics and quality awards, thereby forcing the CEO to act quickly to align business metrics, improvement programs, capabilities, and infrastructure investments with true customer values. The CEO subsequently replaced the previous "inside-out" view of customer value with an "outside-in" view, so that the utility delivered what customers actually wanted. This required dramatic steps to change company capabilities and processes. In particular, the focus shifted from *shorter* outages to *fewer* outages, and (finally) to improving customer satisfaction by providing what the *customers* defined as important.

In the case of a major financial services firm offering mutual funds, financial planning, and similar products and services, the customer played a key role from the beginning. When the company set out to draft a more competitive vision for the IT infrastructure, the CEO went beyond his immediate inclination to "convene five or six of our best people" to draft the vision. He started with an "outside-in" perspective aimed at identifying what *customers* defined as an ideal provider of financial services, rather than what *management* defined. The customer-driven vision was applied to specific processes and capabilities. The company then developed an IT strategy that aligned and linked support elements with that vision.

The CEO used the voice of the customer to both act and persuade. He amended the business mission/vision to encompass important customer needs/wants, such as direct access to company products (rather than only through financial planners). To get the necessary total commitment, he presented his IT strategy to the heads of lines of business and to the management board as a customer-defined vision, and as a result he achieved quick consensus. He then kept going. He reengineered key processes that were not meeting customer needs and implemented a new process for direct customer access to company products and services. This resulted in new growth strategies and new, customer-defined company capabilities.

How to Put the Customer First

The "outside-in" approach—whether followed sooner or later—is the nucleus of Customer Value Management (CVM). As an ongoing framework to manage delivery of customer value and satisfaction, CVM has demonstrated its benefits across a broad range of industries and firms by making company expenditures and improvements more effective and profitable. It enables firms to achieve the goal of putting customers at the center of their business and increases profitability by directing resources toward high-value customers.

CVM both starts and ends with the customer. It aims to deliver optimal value to customers in a well-structured and proven system for aligning business metrics, improvement programs, capabilities, processes, organization, and infrastructure with *customer-defined* value. It reaches for every firm's goal: to create the kind of business that can deliver to customers what they want.

Based on research, analysis, and extensive consulting experiences with companies throughout the world, CVM has been formulated to direct a firm's vision, strategy, products, and services toward the customer. It is a methodical approach that aligns a firm's infrastructure and capabilities to deliver the specific needs and wants that customers value and that drive their buying behavior (Figure 3-1). CVM has both a present and a future orientation. It establishes the customer's current and future vision of an ideal vendor as the design point for business strategy and investment. It ensures that a firm meets the highest priorities of customers for today and tomorrow.

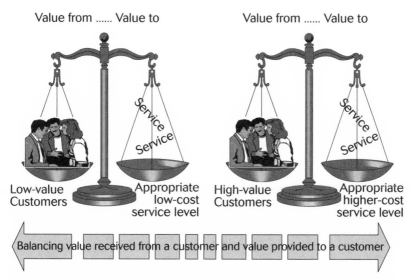

FIGURE 3-1. STRATEGIC ALIGNMENT OF COMPANY AND CUSTOMER VISIONS

CVM addresses the dominant customer problem facing CEOs: how to attract customers and achieve growth in an environment where products and prices are steadily moving closer together among all major competitors. As the traditional bases for differentiation, such as product features and cost, become less significant in setting firms apart, management is forced to look for new ways to gain a competitive edge. For more and more firms, "a winning customer experience" during each interaction with the business is becoming the value proposition. And executives are creating such experiences for their customers in a fluid and volatile customer environment where needs, wants, and perceptions of value change rapidly and continuously.

Rising expectations and demands are not only triggered by direct competitors, but across the board wherever consumers or companies have a buying experience. What one industry provides, customers subsequently expect from other industries. Frequent fliers bring their expectations for service to the Hertz counter and from there to the

Marriott check-in. If customers don't need to stand in line at the car rental, they expect the same service at the hotel and so on down the marketplace chain. To their detriment, many companies have been slow to recognize this "universalization" of expectations. They have a tunnel vision of what customers expect. They risk losing track of the changing nature of "ideal value delivery" and failing to align the firm's actual capabilities and offerings with customer demands. In this environment, building customer loyalty and attracting additional market share requires making the customer's vision an integral part of the business design. CVM enables a firm to become "No. 1 in the eyes of the customer" by ensuring that processes and services are designed to deliver ideal, customer-defined value.

Customer Value Management has demonstrated its benefits across a broad range of industries in both products and services, making a major difference in:

- **Growth**—targeting desired segments, identifying their drivers of buyer behavior, and aligning/linking business process capabilities and infrastructure;
- **Differentiation and competition on value** (rather than on product or price)—delivering customer-defined ideal value at each product or service interaction;
- **Investments**—adding the customer view to planned investments in new infrastructure, such as IT, to make the company more attractive to customers;
- **Channels**—establishing distribution channels that are customer-defined as ideal, thereby attracting customers and increasing market share;
- **Efficiency**—identifying and meeting customer needs in any new process or service that is being redesigned to reduce costs;
- **Customer satisfaction and loyalty**—identifying, measuring, and delivering what's important to the customer and what drives buying behavior. It's important to avoid the pitfall of viewing all metrics on customer satisfaction as equal. U.S. luxury car makers fell into this trap when customers reported that they were "highly satisfied" with the cleanliness of service departments

and the comfort of waiting room lounges. Many of these same customers went out and bought luxury imports, such as a Lexus or Infiniti. The surveys were right in measuring satisfaction levels, but off the mark in understanding the important influencers of the decision to buy. They did not pinpoint the right measures, the ones that make a difference. A comfortable lounge chair in the waiting room is not nearly as significant to the car buyer as a more comfortable driver's seat.

- **Customer profitability management**—attaining a profitable balance between the value provided to a customer and the value a company receives from a customer. This is another area in which CVM can make a significant contribution to the firm. It differentiates high-value from low-value customers and directs resources toward the customers who produce the most profits for the company. When executives are introduced to this concept, they're typically shocked to realize that most customers receive a common, homogeneous level of service, even though not all of the customers are equally profitable. The value provided to customers should be proportionate to their profitability from the company's standpoint. It's a matter of directing resources not to all potential customers to the same degree, but of directing *more* resources to those customers who can produce more profit.

What we're talking about is a twofold differentiation: differentiation of value offered by the firm to the customer, based upon differentiation of value provided by the customer. With CVM, management makes decisions that are based on profitability. Does the cost of delivering value to the customer produce profits that warrant the cost? The decision making balances *value to* the customer against *value from* the customer for the company. This sets CVM apart as a method for managing customer profitability by identifying customers as high or low future value and then delivering cost-efficient customer needs.

CVM provides for the managed delivery of appropriate value to the appropriate customer. This requires an analysis to identify the needs, wants, and values that make an actual difference in each customer's or segment's buying behavior.

Analyzing Value to the Customer

Value to the customer, a well-established feature of modern marketing, wears a new set of clothes in the CVM approach. Its unique "customer value analysis" identifies and prioritizes customer needs and benefits based upon their potential impact upon the business. The analysis, which has been tested and tried successfully worldwide across a wide range of industries, leverages customer needs at each of the "moment of truth" (MOT) interactions that occur during the life cycle of a customer: purchase, delivery, invoicing, post-sales service, etc. MOTs must be analyzed from the customer's perspective to understand the benefits received (or not received) and the combination of benefits that gives a firm the strongest possible competitive advantage.

Moments of truth take on a new meaning and are redefined in CVM. They are traditionally defined as events or encounters in which customers experience satisfaction or dissatisfaction while dealing with a company or with a specific process or service. We have redefined the concept into "moments of potential value." By going beyond what customers want at such moments, we can probe the benefits or value that customers *could* receive—potential value. These occasions constitute opportunities to influence customer behavior and loyalty by providing optimum delivery of value—from a product, service, or process interaction. This value creates demand and a market, and it can differentiate a firm if ideally delivered, using CVM's *outside-in* approach. In mature industries, in which products and prices are becoming increasingly similar, this form of customer-defined service can provide a company with a significant competitive advantage. In more turbulent industries, in which emerging new technologies (such as the Internet) are present, breakthrough delivery of value is possible, unanticipated by customers. This can redefine the industry.

Today's Internet service providers and e-business entrepreneurs need only look to the past for examples of this phenomenon. The widely documented example of the American Airlines Sabre system demonstrates how a company can identify potential value from technology that is recognized by the customer only after its introduction.

During the early days of data processing, customers or their agents had to call each airline in order to understand the full array of flight schedules and ticket prices. An unarticulated customer need existed to be able to easily identify travel alternatives, navigate through them, and select a flight. American Airlines realized it had the technology and the infrastructure to deliver on this offering, creating the Airlines Reservations System. The American Airlines Sabre system for reservations made it possible to locate the best flight schedule or least expensive fare from one city to another. A customer in Newark, New Jersey, for example, could call up and find the best fare to Boise, Idaho, an irresistible customer opportunity that gave birth to a new industry of automation-enabled travel agents. The outcome is dramatized by the bottom line: American Airlines is making more money from Sabre than from flying passengers, a clear case of how to use emerging technology to create new, unanticipated "service" value that surpasses the original "product."[1]

Today, similar opportunities to create totally new value propositions via tailored, personalized services delivered on the Internet have opened up a global marketplace and redefined entire industries. Passive Web sites are becoming interactive, customer-focused, and customized "customer access channels" rather than distribution channels. The customer knowledge captured during these interactions is being used to develop and deliver customer-specific products, services, and information.

Information accessed on the Web, for example, is becoming "advice" rather than data. Instead of a warehouse inventory listing of books, specific titles are suggested based upon the customer's interests or purchasing history and those of similar customers. Instead of generic mass marketing, knowledge of the customer's life cycle, family events, or statistical propensity to buy a next item is used to craft a customer-specific offering. The vehicle (e-business, or other channels for a customer to use) often contains more potential for value delivery to differentiate the vendor than does the product itself.

To play out successfully, both sides of the company-customer equation must come into play. The firm must know itself, its current deliverables, and its possibilities for developing new deliverables, including its capabilities to change and to come up with new offerings. A firm's self-knowledge must be tied to knowledge of customers and their hierarchy of needs, the leverage point at "moments of potential value." Here we have drawn on Maslow's classic hierarchy of needs[2], supplemented by our customer-oriented research, to develop a workable set of three categories for buyer behavior. The categories form a continuum, with "basic needs" at one end and "attractors/differentiators" at the other end. In between are the "satisfiers." Customer value analysis tackles several questions focused on the three categories:

What Are the Basics? "Basic expectations" or "basic needs" must be met or customers will reduce their volume of business or defect to another firm. In terms of Maslow's hierarchy, these are "must haves," the business equivalent of food and shelter. They are a vendor's ticket to play in a particular industry. Failure to provide them sends customers looking for another supplier for their needs. To stay in business, firms must provide a minimum acceptable level of performance. That is how they hold onto customers. The obvious benefit in identifying "basic needs" is to guide the allocation of resources so that they are used where they make the most difference to customers. Under-performance in providing for basic needs drives dissatisfaction and defection. However, over-performing on the basics—such as answering the phone in fewer rings than the competition—does not drive customer behavior or attract additional share. As a general rule, a firm should avoid over-investment in order to be best of breed in basic expectations. Once a firm meets the minimum basics, it should direct any additional resources or funding toward needs for which being the best will attract customers and increase market share.

What Are the Attractors/Differentiators? These are needs that, if well satisfied, prompt existing customers to remain with a firm as well as attract new customers away from competitors. These needs parallel the upper levels of Maslow's hierarchy, providing the business equivalent of self-actualization and fulfillment. They make a difference that counts with customers, they differentiate vendors, and they provide an incentive for customers to leave one firm and take their business to another. Attractors are at the core of competitive formulas for success and must be viewed in terms of performance gaps between a firm and its competition. Investments should go to attractors to provide best-of-breed delivery, once the basics have been met.

What Are the Satisfiers? Whereas *basic needs* make a difference in holding customers and *attractors* have an impact on gaining them, *satisfiers* improve the way customers feel about a firm. But they do not make or break relationships; they are desirable but not necessary, and they lack the power to drive customer behavior toward or away from a firm. Satisfiers are positive add-ons that neither create loyalty nor cause attrition. Their usefulness in CVM is in separating what features or services receive a positive rating from those that make a significant buying difference. This awareness avoids the experience of U.S. luxury car makers with their clean service areas and comfortable lounges, accompanied by the paradox of lost sales. At Wal-Mart, a greeter at the door who directs customers toward their shopping target is an obvious satisfier. The same with banks that add the friendliness feature of knowing your name. Such features might rate at the top of the charts in surveys of customer satisfaction, but they don't individually cause customers to leave if they are not provided or to change vendors if available elsewhere[3] (Figure 3-2).

As tools of analysis, these categories enable firms to identify which combination of customer needs—basic needs, satisfiers, or

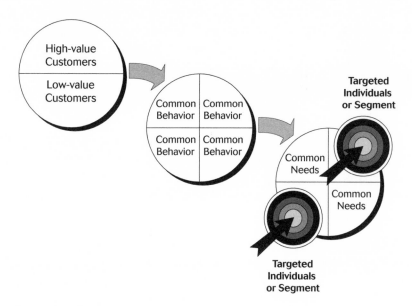

FIGURE 3-2. DIFFERENTIATION OF VALUE

attractors—provides the strongest competitive advantage (by avoiding or containing attrition or by maximizing attraction and retention of customers through differentiation). What counts is what drives customer buying behavior. The analysis identifies where customers perceive performance gaps between a firm and its competitors on features that help them make up their minds. It also leads to informed estimates on how customer buying behavior would change if performance gaps were removed, and it points management in the right direction when changing or adding new products and services.[4]

If a firm is ahead of its competitors, then the analysis would focus on whether the firm is over-delivering in areas that don't increase loyalty or don't connect with attractors. On the other hand, if attractors are involved, then moving further ahead in these areas might make business sense, after factoring in the cost and the potential response from competition. Here we're describing a portfolio approach to customers' basic needs—offering attractors and satisfiers in order to apply a strategy that produces the greatest return in a competitive marketplace. For example, if a firm is lagging behind the competition in meeting basic expectations (and therefore losing customers) or in drawing attractors (not building more business from customers and not attracting new ones), management must decide which mix of basic needs and attractors will best serve the firm's profit-making goals. One strategy might focus on meeting minimum basic needs for all current and future targeted customers while investing selectively in attractors that will appeal to a particular segment of highly profitable, high-value customers (Figure 3-2).

Customer Value Management establishes a practical framework for making critical decisions about which set of benefits to deliver, to which customers, and with what reasonable expectations of significant results. There are a variety of techniques to gather value information to help implement CVM.

Market Segmentation. To benefit fully from market segmentation, firms must combine customer profiles and transaction data with purchased outside databases. They must mine this information to discover clusters of customers and prospects with similar attributes and buying behavior. By probing the clusters, the company can identify common underlying values that account for similar behavior and can be used to develop a customer-defined company vision. The relevant questions are: Who are the customers? What drives their behavior? Whom do we wish to attract? Whom do we wish to retain? How do we appeal to them? What is their value to the company? The answers to these questions enable management to differentiate high-value and low-value customers and target particular niches. Once customers are targeted, the firm can map crucial ingredients of common behavior and common needs for profitable segmentation.

A refining process can narrow the segments into precise targets. Once high- and low-value customers are identified, the firm can identify different customer sets within those larger categories. The customers can be segmented by their buying habits, such as time of year that they purchase items and their choices of products. The narrowing goes on and on in terms of similar buying behaviors, which are based on common values, needs, and wants and translated into price, product, and service. Firms cannot realistically (and profitably) be all things for all potential customers at all times, but they can offer the right thing at the right time for the right customers (Figure 3-3).

Market Research. The critical focus in market research is on understanding what customers value and then securing the customer's vision of ideal delivery of that value. Of course, companies should

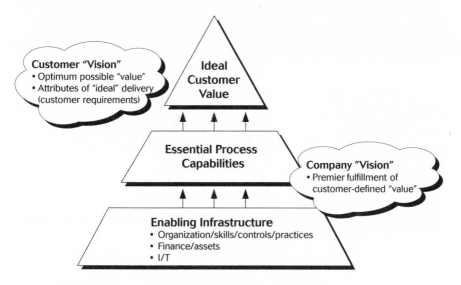

FIGURE 3-3. SEGMENTING AND TARGETING CUSTOMERS

not limit market segmentation and research to their own customers; rather, they should also include the customers of competitors, who represent the marketplace. As a supplement, quantitative research identifies current importance and performance ratings, pinpoints gaps between the company and the competition, and supports investment and resource decisions. The boom in Internet buying has added a new dimension to market research by enabling vendors to gather significant amounts of real-time customer data, providing further impetus for CVM.[5]

Benchmarks. Firms should measure delivery of value to customers by using wide-ranging benchmarks that include an international perspective in line with the global marketplace the customer is now experiencing. Internally, benchmarks identify "best" business units that are performing significantly better than others. Externally, they measure performance within and across industries and should take into account the fact that customer perceptions of a firm are influenced by all buying and service experiences. Today, virtually all other companies and industries are a potential source of benchmarking, just as customer expectations can be set by other industries. For example, extraordinary service by an auto dealer (such as a loaner automobile while yours is in the shop) can trigger similar expectations of service in other industries (such as a loaner computer).

Brainstorming and Invention. Brainstorming by the business functions that comprise a service process can lead to major breakthroughs in the delivery of ideal value to customers. It develops joint understanding of customers' needs, generates cross-functional buy-in of what the firm must do for the customer, and optimizes cross-value chain capabilities By "cross-value chain capabilities," we mean delivering offerings to customers in various forms, channels of distribution, and new forms different from what the firm might have done in the past. In the give-and-take of cross-functional brainstorming, managers in different functions, processes, and units begin to understand their collective relationships and their mutual impact on deliverables. Typically, an executive will comment after a CVM brainstorming session, "This was the first time that we have actually met as a cross-functional team to solve a common issue."

One feature stands out in CVM: the ability, metaphorically, to pin "the voice of the customer" on the wall. It can be the single most powerful element in reengineering or in transforming a diverse organization or a value chain. A strong case for action emerges when a process-oriented team rallies around fulfilling the customer's vision of ideal delivery. That is the essence of the "outside-in" approach: identifying the *customer's vision* of optimum value and its attributes. The *company vision* then aligns business capabilities and infrastructure with the *customer vision* so that company deliverables match customer demand (as shown in Figure 3-1).

Management can go further. By understanding the reasons why customers have particular needs and the values/benefits underlying them, planning teams often formulate unique combinations of capabilities or existing competencies that go beyond what customers foresee or articulate. These become the source of breakthroughs.

The CVM Difference

Customer Value Management does more than keep the customer in the picture when a firm makes a move to change, expand, or meet a new competitive challenge. It converts the customer into a "partner," from the planning to the execution stage. When a firm plans a major investment or change in its infrastructure, the customer is factored in as the ultimate judge and jury for the outcome. Often, the external nature of planned changes will direct the management team toward Customer Value Management—for example, when market share or customer satisfaction is the catalyst for change.

However, when a firm is downsizing or making other more internally driven changes, then the impact on the customer is also crucial to the consequences. When the driver of change and the focus are internal, management must beware of forgetting its customers. The customers do not immediately come to the fore when companies make plans to cut costs, reduce defects, or reorganize IT. But whatever the firm does will eventually affect customers and their reactions to the firm. Not only does it make sense to avoid alienating customers by the impact of changes upon them, but look-ahead firms find ways to increase their market appeal in the way customers experience the

Bringing in the Customer Belatedly

A global petrochemical company's order-to-invoice process in Asia faced a clearly defined problem: the cost and quality of order fulfillment fell short of business objectives and failed to deliver customer satisfaction. The company's response was complicated when management started with reengineering rather than Customer Value Management, as often happens.

The company identified its core processes and set up process owners and cross-functional teams to identify and implement improvements. After devising several engineering options, the teams faced the challenge of deciding which possible actions would meet customer needs. When the firm introduced Customer Value Management into decision making at that point, management found that its existing customer satisfaction surveys lacked what was needed for effective CVM (customer-defined questions that probed areas of actual value to the customers). This prompted a fast-path effort to commission customer roundtables with CVM experts, who worked with front-line staff to identify customer needs, underlying values, and priorities. These, in turn, were used (albeit belatedly) to validate or revise the reengineering team's designs—from the customer's perspective. The reason staff could be queried instead of customers is that the firm already had a rich body of customer input data upon which staff members could base their attitudes and conclusions

As a result, when the reengineering team subsequently presented its 20-plus recommendations to the board, each was anchored in the perspective of the customer as well as the cost factor and company benefits. The board approved all the recommendations and the CVM approach became a critical first step not only in reengineering the order-to-invoice process, but also in transforming the entire enterprise along customer-focused lines. The key decision taken was to inject customer perspectives into future activities, leaving to the management team to determine how best to solicit customer opinions consequences of internal changes, whether in lower prices, improved services, or greater choices. If a five-year plan is in the making, sound planning calls for envisioning customer expectations and reaction by asking, *What would make the business an ideal provider?* Once management has addressed the customer issue, it is on firm ground to define the capabilities and underlying infrastructure, including IT, required to carry out the company's strategy.

By going beyond the normal practice of merely measuring customer satisfaction, CVM uses the customer view to engineer new value propositions, to develop new standards and capabilities, and to define infrastructure requirements. Three brief examples demonstrate the versatility of the CVM framework in these areas.

A customer orientation can reveal opportunities that are not tied to a firm's products, as in the case of a pharmaceutical company faced with increasing competition from other leading producers, including those with generic products. Research into the company's relationships with doctors identified many market segments that wanted easier and more responsive sales and service relationships. If the company delivered on this "value," the doctors were prepared to buy more of its products at existing (profitable) prices. The next step paid off. The company focused on customer service and sales-order-entry processes and on the information and telecommunication systems that supported both. When these systems were reconfigured to meet customer values in a pilot market segment, sales increased substantially within only a few months.

When a credit card company wanted to establish new standards of performance for call centers, benchmarking was both local and global. Initially, the company explored metrics based on top-performing banks, with the aim of proposing them as standards to its association of member banks. Besides the limitation of having a narrow focus, this approach faced the handicap of asking banks to adhere to benchmarks set by the competition. Instead, the card company's executive team developed a customer-defined strategy by identifying key customer targets, probing interactions with call centers, and establishing needs, wants, values, and desired levels of service—all from the customer viewpoint.

Don't Just Make Promises to the Customer—Deliver

An internationally renowned hotel chain neglected a critical element of CVM when it undertook an all-out advertising campaign to promise defect-free stays for business travelers. The promise was on target in the value offered to high-value customers, but the other half of the equation—delivery—was lacking: the infrastructure was simply not in place to provide what was promised.

The gap was underscored by the experience of an international executive who checked into one of the chain's hotels in response to the ad campaign. First, the hotel had no record of his reservation, though it did manage to find him a room. Second, the ceiling light did not work, though a bedside lamp did work (illuminating a placard promising a defect-free stay). Third, the television did not work. As the executive reported after he confronted the hotel manager: "The manager confessed that there were actually no new capabilities to perform at the defect-free level nor any procedures to deal effectively with customer complaints when defects did occur. He said that no new training, personnel programs, or reservations systems had been deployed at that point to generate improved performance."

So the customer-driven effort backfired. The chain had raised the expectations of a high-value customer segment and then created dissatisfaction by not introducing the processes, capabilities, and infrastructure to deliver on its customer promise.

The company went even further. It identified firms inside and outside the industry that provided distinguished service and researched their specific capabilities and enabling infrastructure. In addition, the company encouraged member banks to survey their own customers to identify local perceptions, needs, and wants so that the banks could identify the right mix of services for their particular markets and customize their offerings. By using the CVM approach, the credit card company was able to establish an actionable call center strategy that identified what customers wanted and how to deliver it. The strategy became part of an educational package for members and was used with significant success in North America and Asia to provide consistent customer service and maintain a brand image.

In the case of a major high-technology company exploring a huge new market in China, top management had a limited local infrastructure and needed to identify, prioritize, and manage the critical success factors involved in developing the market. Its country management team used CVM analysis to identify the "must haves" for the market and the required capabilities and infrastructure. This enabled the company to get the most out of what was available and develop resource plans for the key infrastructure elements that would determine success. By using a customer focus, a cross-functional management team was able to settle complex issues quickly and make decisions that responded to the market.[6]

When Is CVM Appropriate?

While our consulting experience shows that different driving forces and situations move firms toward the customer value approach, the common denominator is a realization that a firm's internally focused processes do not deliver what customers need and want. Specifically, CVM is appropriate when firms:

- find that the gap in products and prices between them and their competitors is narrowing and they want to differentiate and compete on the value delivered by *optimum* services;
- provide commodities and set out to minimize cost and compete on price by identifying and delivering *minimum* needs;
- pursue growth by attracting new customers or by attracting more spending by existing customers;
- want to optimize a channel by making it "ideal" to customers to increase market share;
- seek to optimize a multi-enterprise value chain (suppliers, the firm, channels);
- modify or redesign internal processes to meet the minimum requirements of low-value customers while being selectively attractive to high-value customers;
- encourage customers to use lower-cost processes, services, or channels by removing "inhibitors" and adding "attractors"—

thereby reducing costs and increasing revenues;

- plan improvements in the infrastructure, such as IT, and get the most out of improvements by ensuring that the changes also make the firm more attractive to customers;
- target desired customers when customer dissatisfaction and attrition are issues and ensure that they build "must have" requirements into processes to remove the causes of dissatisfaction.

Putting CVM into Action

The actual scope and speed of a firm's move toward CVM varies, depending on the company's position in the marketplace, the type of industry in which it competes, and what the competition is doing. When technology is moving very fast and is driving customer needs, the top customer priority is for *products that perform better, faster, and more reliably than any others currently available*. This is evident in industries like personal computer software, online services, and aircraft manufacturing.[7] When a company is competing in such a fast-moving marketplace, CVM can produce high dividends, particularly in deploying new technologies. It monitors changing customer needs and identifies ways to utilize the technologies to produce unprecedented delivery of value.

A different situation faces companies operating in stable markets with common and competitive products. When products and price move close together, a firm's strategy changes for retaining loyal customers and attracting new ones. A CVM approach can offer protection against falling behind by helping a company identify and deliver what customers value beyond price and product. One powerful answer is to set the company apart in services in every customer interaction. A company can deliver a competitive difference by reengineering service capabilities or by drawing on third-party members of the extended value chain. This happens with utilities, fixed telecommunications, automotive firms, airlines, and retailers—relatively mature markets in which new technologies are available to all participants from third-party suppliers.

In such markets, a new entrant can change the rules of the game by using technology to create a new value proposition for the customer. A startup insurance company did just that when it found that customers would buy policies directly by phone rather than through agents if the value proposition was right. So the company set up a world-class combination of call center technology and practice, laser printing, and customer database management to deliver faster, better, and cheaper service than was previously available to insurance buyers. The breakthrough value delivery differentiated the company in service and propelled it to market leadership in its category within five years.

In either context—a rapidly changing industry or a relatively stable one—management can use CVM in a *top-down* scenario or a *bottom-up* scenario. In the case of the startup insurance company, the scenario started at the bottom by identifying and using technology to create an infrastructure that created an offering providing customer value. Internet services providers, as noted earlier, are well positioned to use emerging technology to envision (*bottom-up CVM*) such creative new delivery of service value. (In the Figure 3-3 pyramid, this represents leveraging the enabling infrastructure to create new capabilities and customer value.) This *bottom-up* scenario has three elements:

- capitalizing on emerging technologies,
- developing innovative capabilities, and
- providing deliverables that redefine value propositions and attractors.[8]

A *top-down* scenario begins with understanding customer needs and wants. A company identifies "ideal customer value" (top of the pyramid in Figure 3-3) and designs its infrastructure and processes to deliver on the "ideal." When the Japanese introduced this approach several years ago, it was called Quality Function Deployment and it was used to design products, notably cars. Ford used the approach to design and develop the Taurus, which became America's top-selling car. The customer designed the outcome and drove the changes in process and enabling infrastructure. In the process or service arena, this can mean developing bank and other financial statements that meet customer specifications of what's easy to read, or an ATM machine or kiosk that is user-friendly. Today, a powerful top-down application of CVM is to have customers define an outside-in vision of ideal "e-access" to your business, creating a customer-defined access channel (rather than an inside-out distribution channel).

Keeping CVM Going

CVM aligns a company's resources, skills, and leadership with the customer vision of *ideal value delivery*. Fully implemented, it integrates and links the needs and behavior of the customers, the suppliers, and the company into the value chain. This is an undertaking whose elements are manifold: customer and prospect segmentation based on profitability; actionable, needs-based market research linked to business reengineering and process design; organizational design; cultural alignment; sustained change management; benchmarking; and development and deployment of information technology at the customer interface and throughout the value chain.[9]

In our experience, few organizations possess these elements at world-class level, so management goes outside the firm to implement CVM, either for a single process or for the entire business. It's important to emphasize that CVM is not a one-time exercise. It is an ongoing proposition, because the day after a CVM project is completed or a process put in place, a company is "one day out of touch with customers." All the variables of the marketplace are in play. Customers' requirements and perceptions continually change in terms of needs and wants and in terms of what your competitors are doing. Management must stay on top of complaints, track customer service, identify and prioritize opportunities, and adjust business plans and actions. This calls for continuous monitoring of customer requirements and changes in company offerings to keep pace with the requirements.

Rather than a one-shot or quick-fix approach to the global marketplace, with its rapid and continuous change, CVM enables a firm to maintain a continuous customer focus that both protects and expands its customer base. Given the exigencies of today's marketplace, the axiom about never taking the customer for granted has never been truer—and the penalty for neglecting or not knowing the customer has never been so severe. Customers can be here today and gone tomorrow. They require constant attention. See how they run. Find out what *they* want and need by managing in terms of *their* values (see Figure 3-4).

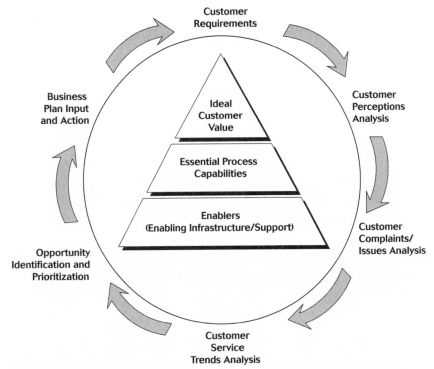

FIGURE 3-4. ONGOING CUSTOMER VALUE MANAGEMENT PROCESSES

Summary

Companies have always talked about putting customers at the center of their business. But too often, this has been more rhetoric than reality, more intention than implementation. Customer Value Management enables companies to profit from serving customer wants and needs by identifying and managing customer knowledge while simultaneously balancing the practical business interests of the firm. With CVM, companies can develop and implement a customer-defined vision of ideal value delivery and put into action the required client service standards, process capabilities, and enabling infrastructure. Customer value becomes both a reality check and a stimulus for converting information into profit-generating knowledge.

This approach is part of an enterprise-wide commitment to knowledge and its development, management, and leveraging—the subject of the next three chapters in Part Two.

For Further Reading

Sheila Kessler, *Measuring and Managing Customer Satisfaction: Going for the Gold* (Milwaukee: ASQ Quality Press, 1996).

This is a "nuts and bolts," how-to process guide for understanding and tracking customer opinions about the goods and services of any business; one of the better such tool kits.

Harvey Thompson (with Merlin Stone), *Close to the Customer* (Bedford, United Kingdom: Policy Publications, 1997); "What Do Your Customers Really Want?" *Journal of Business Strategy*, August 1998.

These publications provide a concise overview of Customer Value Management and the management issues involved.

Harvey Thompson, *The Customer-Centered Enterprise: How IBM and Other World-Class Companies Achieve Extraordinary Results by Putting Customers First* (New York: McGraw-Hill, 2000).

This book provides the most complete exploration available on CVM, what it is, and how to implement it.

Ron Zemke and John A. Woods, *Best Practices in Customer Service* (Amherst, MA: HRD Press, 1998 and New York: AMACOM, 1999).

This is an anthology with over 30 articles on how to deliver superior customer service along with several case studies of customer-focused corporate initiatives written by those implementing them; a process- and quality-focused view.

Part Two

LEADING THROUGH KNOWLEDGE

Managing Knowledge: Issues and Implications

> Learning is not compulsory.
> Neither is survival.
> —W. Edwards Deming

By managing knowledge, firms are capitalizing on a major asset that in the recent past they have taken for granted and left greatly underutilized. In the 1990s, knowledge management has become a top priority as work increases in complexity, workforce demographics change drastically, computing becomes universal, and intangible outcomes predominate. This chapter defines knowledge management and addresses the issues firms are facing, such as collaboration and consistency, product and process innovation, and information overload.

An example of how a little knowledge can go a long (and profitable) way started at a Singapore conference on artificial fabrics, where a manager from a global chemical and fabric manufacturer collected a stack of product literature and stuffed it into his briefcase. He included a brochure from a South Korean firm on a very specific type of artificial fabric.

Back in his office, the manager told two colleagues about the

The lead writers of this chapter are Laurence Prusak and Eric Lesser.

conference, the trip, and the Korean-made fabric, starting an information chain reaction that led to usable knowledge.

A colleague, who was active in a company chat network, shared the information about the product with his Intranet community. A member of that community printed out the item and put it in his briefcase on the off chance that someone in the company might be interested in the product. Three months later, while he was on a plane trip with a senior executive, the technology for the fabric came up in an informal discussion and the executive remarked, "We ought to look into it."

"Wait a minute," said his companion. "There's a Korean firm licensing that exact technology." He pulled the item about the South Korean fabric out of his bag and showed it to him. Two months later, at an upper management meeting on new products and licensing opportunities, the same technology came up in a discussion. The executive reported that one of his people had learned about a Korean firm that developed the technology. The company chairman jumped at the information and sent two executives to Korea to look into the fabric. They liked what they saw, negotiated a license to produce the fabric, and the manufacturer went to market with a product using the process.

The fabric merits a knowledge-based label: "Developed in South Korea, Discovered in an Information Exchange, Made in the United States." The labyrinthine example drives home the point that knowledge becomes a firm's usable asset when both formal and informal structures are in play to exchange information and make it usable as knowledge. Fundamentally, as in this example, people are the learners, structures and systems the enablers. Because knowledge is not automatic and not always predictable, management must support a fertile environment in which information is shared and learning takes place. It must also provide technology enablers such as the Intranet and chat networks. Fundamentally, managing knowledge means managing an environment that optimizes sharing, exchanging, and learning.

The concept of using knowledge in a firm is hardly new, but there is a significant difference today. Up until now, there was less of a need for the explicit management of knowledge. Companies normally let knowledge go its unpredictable way, taking it for granted that there always would be enough to provide competitive advantage.

This is no longer the case. The company that doesn't focus on knowledge as a major asset and capitalize upon it is at a serious competitive disadvantage.[1] From the corner copier store to the global car manufacturer, knowledge makes the difference for today and tomorrow in how successfully firms stand up against competition—whether it be across the street or across the ocean—and how well they serve their customers. Knowledge management has become a top priority for whoever is in charge throughout an organization—at the top and at all levels.

To remind yourself of how knowledge has captured attention, take a second look at what has appeared in the business press and journals and at what keynote speakers have proclaimed at conventions and conferences. In print and at the podium, a focus on knowledge invokes the familiar mantra about the accelerating pace of change. Stable business environments are disappearing, opportunities rise and fall in a flash, "Web years" are now measured in months as the life span of new technology gets shorter by the week. Executives don't need to be told about the tidal wave of change. They want collaboration and consistency in their operations, innovation in their products and services, and productive use of information. The more they recognize these needs, the more they value knowledge as the new wealth of organizations.

What Is Knowledge?

To get a perspective on what's happening in firms and what needs to be done, begin with a clear fix on knowledge in organizations. Knowledge is the collection of experiences, heuristics, values, and cognitive frames that are in the minds of individuals. It's important to emphasize that knowledge originates in people and depends on people to use it to produce outcomes. Knowledge is in individuals; it's embedded in work activities, and it's deposited in documents and reports. Every firm has knowledge, though few firms exploit its full potential. For too many firms, knowledge is idle capital. The memorable comment of Hewlett-Packard CEO Lew Platt about his own firm resonates throughout all firms: "If HP knew what HP knows, we would be three times as profitable."[2]

Knowledge is more than data or information. Data is a record of a transaction, usually stored in a system. Obviously you need data to run any business, but it is the lowest level of content, like reading the phone book with its arbitrary collection of listings in alphabetical order. The phone book does not tell you what to ask for and how to find out what you need to know.

At the next level—information—the sender transmits a message to the receiver. It is one way traffic. Picasso's "Guernica" is a message. Love songs, Robert Frost poems, and white papers are messages as well. All in their own way "form" the minds of receivers by changing the way they understand things, leaving it to the receivers to determine how they are informed by messages.

The characteristics of knowledge make it valuable—and also difficult to manage. As defined in collaboration with Professor Thomas H. Davenport of Boston University, here is a characteristic-based definition of knowledge:

A fluid mix of framed experience, values, contextual information, and expert insight that provides a framework for evaluating and incorporating new experiences and information. It originates and is applied in the minds of knowers. In organizations, it often becomes embedded not only in documents or repositories, but also in organizational routines, processes, practices, and norms.[3]

Knowledge emerges from information when the outcomes of interchanges are collected, organized, and stored in the minds of individuals who identify patterns and find meanings that make a usable difference. Over time, the learning process becomes the stock and trade of an organization as it becomes embedded in routines, processes, and work norms. Knowledge then becomes more visible and more available. It becomes a shared asset. In this way, what individuals learn and know becomes part of how the organization operates and produces outcomes (Figure 4-1). This is the essence of "working knowledge."[4]

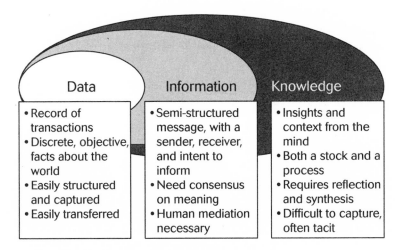

Data	Information	Knowledge
• Record of transactions • Discrete, objective, facts about the world • Easily structured and captured • Easily transferred	• Semi-structured message, with a sender, receiver, and intent to inform • Need consensus on meaning • Human mediation necessary	• Insights and context from the mind • Both a stock and a process • Requires reflection and synthesis • Difficult to capture, often tacit

FIGURE 4-1. DATA, INFORMATION, AND KNOWLEDGE

Why Knowledge? Why Now?

Four reasons, in particular, explain the increasing importance of workplace knowledge:

1. Growing Complexity of Work. As knowledge has become a key factor of production within industries and firms, an updated perspective on work has emerged—work as a knowledge-based activity. The demand for knowledge shows up everywhere in the workplace. Stockbrokers are no longer out there just taking orders for stocks or pursuing customers at the friendly 19th hole. They are financial services consultants who are helping clients achieve financial goals. When brokerage houses call the troops together for early-morning briefings, they push knowledge-based services as a vehicle for building business and for beating off the competition for their clients.

Even a neighborhood photocopying business needs knowledgeable employees who know how to customize the technology to the individual needs of customers coming in off the street. As people work more and more in teams, they take on new duties and tasks; to do so, they need access to knowledge that is already available. Otherwise, they continually reinvent the wheel—or spin their wheels.

Complexity makes escalating demands for all firms. The more complex work becomes, the less likely that one or two individuals

can know enough to master an operation. Complexity also com-
pounds the likelihood that something will go "wrong" and will
require specialized knowledge to fix.[5] In either case, the knowledge
needed is often tacit and found only in the know-how and work
methods of individuals and groups of technicians or professionals. To
operate efficiently, organizations need access to knowledge that is
articulated only partially or not at all. For the most part, though,
organizations still depend on very informal processes, if not sheer
luck, to get knowledge where it is needed when people need it.

2. Workforce Changes and Trends. The chief knowledge officer of
a professional services organization pinpointed the impact of workforce changes with a stunning statistic: 25 percent of the people in
his firm were in either their first or their last year of employment.
This phenomenon is widespread. People are coming on board without experience at the same time that people with the most experience
are leaving. Early retirement joins rightsizing, downsizing, mergers,
and consolidations in depleting the ranks of the experienced, the seasoned, and the knowledgeable. This creates a serious gap and a formidable management problem. On the one hand, firms must retain
knowledge while losing people who have it; on the other hand, they
must make knowledge available to people who still have not acquired
it and need it sooner rather than later. The traffic in knowledge is
moving in the wrong direction: knowledge is going out the door
much faster than it is coming in.

In the age of "free agent" employees, the departure of top performers adds to the problem. The best and brightest are recruited by
other firms and headhunters. These employees are always ready to
listen to outside offers, since their loyalty is increasingly to their
careers rather than to their companies, and their focus is on employ-
ability rather than employment by a particular company. Outsiders,
such as consultants and outsourcers, add to the knowledge "flight"
when they arrive with strategic knowledge, tailor it to the firm, and
then take it away—unless firms have a knowledge-oriented policy
that captures, retains, and incorporates outsider knowledge.

At Harvard Pilgrim Health Care, a major Boston-area HMO, management backed up its emphasis on knowledge as an asset by putting a
price tag on it. Both incoming and departing staffers answer knowledge-

oriented questions (about the components of their jobs, the knowledge needed, "secret code words and procedures," how a job fits into various processes, etc.). The answers are presented to a panel of senior managers and peers who evaluate their worth; the company then pays a bonus of $1,000 to $5,000, depending on the quality level of the knowledge. For newcomers, the policy demonstrates how much the company values knowledge. And with respect to departing staffers, the policy enables the company to retain knowledge that would otherwise leave with them.[6]

3. Omnipresence of Computing. The spread of computing to every part of the workplace continues at a rapid rate (as discussed in Chapters 1 and 2), with no sign of a slowdown as more and more applications are developed to work with faster, smaller, more powerful computer chips. A major unintended consequence of this expansion is that cheaper and easier to use computing puts a higher premium on workplace expertise. This happens in two ways.

First, the computer is seen less as an information machine and much more as a workplace utility, especially with the convergence of communications and storage capacities. By 1998, more than 90 percent of new PCs sold were equipped to communicate with networks, such as the Internet. Using computers to gain knowledge, rather than to house information, is an important workplace development. It accounts for the rapid deployment of Intranets and the spectacular growth of Internet usage. As work becomes more complex, workers use the computer right at hand to find the answers they need to do their work and to solve problems. The wired-up desktop that is tied to information-rich networks exemplifies a ready-made response to the complex demands of the workplace.

Second, the "informing" aspects of computing work, as noted by Shoshana Zuboff over a decade ago,[7] draw on the dual nature of a computer: it can simultaneously manipulate symbols and capture information regarding its own activities, which can then be formatted and distributed. Zuboff contrasts this aspect with "automating," a unidimensional activity focused solely on efficiency. "Informing," in one form or another, contributes to new ways of developing organizational intelligence and information, which adds to the complexity of work and demands particular expertise to make sense of it.

4. Rise of Intangible Outcomes. The rise of intangibles has several important implications for workplace knowledge, starting with the statistics upon which we depend. Our traditional metrics for measurements, valuation and rewards, often are not up to the task of capturing what we know and need to know. These hangovers from the Second Industrial Age focus on tangible inputs and outputs to measure productivity. They fail, however, to keep up with the shift to a knowledge-dependent economy. Measures in such an economy focus on outcome rather than output, on innovation rather than replication, on replenishment rather than gross utilization, on tomorrow rather than yesterday.

We must stress one point in particular in the search for appropriate measurements: knowledge per se in a firm cannot be realistically measured (either in a person or an organizational activity), but firms can measure knowledge-based outcomes and proxies for knowledge optimization. To measure outcomes, firms can focus on patents, new products, innovative work practices, and customer retention. IBM, among others, uses patents as knowledge proxies, while Ford uses the introduction of innovative work processes. Sony and 3M examine knowledge in terms of how many new products they put on the market. Some major banks view customer retention as a function of their customer knowledge.

In addition to measuring outcomes, firms can measure the diffusion and transfer of knowledge in terms of speed and scope of adaptation and observable results. They can also measure knowledge in terms of internal and external replacement value, market valuation, and latent and supplementary value. As firms get a better handle on the value of their own significant knowledge, they will develop more accurate metrics for measuring and rewarding their elusive—and highly valuable—knowledge-based activities.

What Knowledge Issues Do Firms Face?

In theory, organizations can use knowledge management to address any and all choices confronting them. In practice, management has the task of identifying the choices that involve the greatest opportunities, the highest priorities, and the biggest payoffs. Given the reasons for the emergence of knowledge management and the realities of today's fast-changing world, firms looking for knowledge management solutions face the following issues in particular:

- collaboration and consistency,
- product and process innovation,
- information overload.

Collaboration and Consistency. The more firms spread out their work and tasks, the greater are the difficulties they face in getting the parts to work together and the more inconsistent their operations can become. The issue of collaboration and consistency arises in both products and services. A manufacturing company with plants in different locations and countries, for example, faces differences in production and quality from one plant to another. How can the best practices of one plant benefit a laggard operation halfway across the country or around the world? A retail bank operation with multiple locations in the same city finds that some branches are flourishing while others are falling behind. What can the organization do about it? An oil company that drills around the world inevitably faces breakdowns in remote locations. Similar problems, similar demands on oil company expertise, but different outcomes in making repairs. How does know-how that works on a rig in the North Sea apply to a rig in the Gulf of Mexico?

A number of factors are typically at work. Globalization has scattered operations around the country and the globe and, as a result, has scattered expertise as well. Meanwhile, outsourcers, telecommuters, project only staffers, and consultants appear and disappear, and companies certainly cannot assume that these workers will be where they're wanted when needed. Increasingly, as work is parceled out to teams and divided into projects, even being located under the same headquarters roof does not guarantee collaboration. Teams in the same location can be less likely to get together than teams scattered around the globe, who are reminded by geography that they need to build and maintain bridges over physical separation.

When firms flatten their structures, an atmosphere of isolation works its way insidiously into the environment. Decentralization breeds separation as units feel encouraged to go their own way. They may even compete against each other as much as with other firms, prompted by invidious comparisons that top management makes and prodded by reward systems based on top-performing units.

More and more, meanwhile, managers are asking, "Where have all my people gone?" They see their employees less and less. Permanent staffers telecommute and work at satellite and customer locations. Temporary staffers come and go as projects begin and end. Outsourcing firms send a parade of people to handle a particular job without getting connected to a company or its managers. Consultants, often from multiple firms, appear and disappear, leaving behind results and reports.

While such fragmentation is avoidable, knowledge, when shared, can become the glue that holds units and people together. When well-managed, it becomes the cohesive force that makes both collaboration and consistency possible. When a company deploys best practices across the firm, people apply knowledge to produce results. Managers can find answers to questions that bedevil all managements in the face of complexity, dispersion, and inconsistent results. Why, for example, do some customer service reps meet customer needs better than others do? What do they do that's different or special? Or why and how do soft drink bottling operations vary from one plant to the next? How can all plants achieve similar high levels of productivity? In most cases, the issue comes down to the same or similar tasks performed by different actors with different results.

When British Petroleum confronted the issue of collaboration and consistency, it established a Virtual Teamwork Program. The knowledge-based thinking behind the effort is unequivocal. "Knowledge, ideas, and innovative solutions are being diffused throughout the world today at a speed that would have been unimaginable 10 or 20 years ago," CEO John Browne asserts. "Companies are only now learning how to go beyond seeing that movement as a threat to seeing it as an opportunity. We see it as a tremendous opportunity.

"Learning is at the heart of a company's ability to adapt to a rapidly changing environment. It is the key to being able both to identify opportunities that others might not see and to exploit those opportunities rapidly and fully."[8]

The Virtual Teamwork Program enabled teams to collaborate across different locations in British Petroleum's exploration division, which finds and produces oil and gas. The aim, which succeeded, was to draw on what 42 units around the world know and to spread their wealth of knowledge. The company drew on technology as an enabler: desktop videoconferencing, multimedia e-mail, application sharing, document scanners, shared chalkboards, tools to record video clips, groupware, and a Web browser. Coaches (as opposed to trainers) worked with the members of scattered teams on using the technology and on mastering the process of sharing knowledge with each other. The process virtually duplicated the face-to-face exchange, which is at the heart of knowledge exchange.

There is nothing like examples of how the program succeeded to convince participants and everyone else at British Petroleum of the benefits of collaboration. When operations on a North Sea mobile drilling ship came to a halt in 1995, the engineers on board didn't need to wait for an expert to be flown in by helicopter, nor did they need to bring the ship back to port. They set up the faulty hardware in front of a video camera connected to a BP Virtual Teamwork Station, which in turn dialed via satellite the office of a drilling equipment expert. He examined the faulty part on the screen, diagnosed the problem quickly, and walked the shipboard engineers through the repair. Without that prompt repair, the ship's down time would have cost $150,000 daily (the price of leasing) while an expert was flown out or the ship was brought back to port.

Incidents like this one and the overall benefits of virtual teaming brought requests from throughout British Petroleum to be included (the company set a 1999 target of networking 10,000 PCs). The monitored benefits included a big drop in person hours to solve problems, a decrease in helicopter trips to offshore oil platforms, and a reduction in rework during construction projects because designers, fabricators, construction workers, and operations people could collaborate more effectively.

Product and Process Innovation. A second business issue, innovation, has come to the fore amid the pressure to maintain competitive advantage in a fast-moving, global economy. The game is being played on several fields and is driven by the accelerating rate of technological change. Microsegmentation and mass customization make it necessary to run faster to stay ahead as shrinking life cycles continuously threaten market leaders. Whether the product is corn flakes or PCs, or whether the service is elevator repair or mutual fund offerings, a marketplace leader has no hope of holding position with a stand-pat offering. The sun hardly sets on today's breakthrough before it becomes tomorrow's standard offering.

The demand for quality increases the pressure to innovate, as customers not only want the latest but demand the best at the lowest price. Hence the twofold pressure of higher quality and lower cost. A visit to an Internet chat room illustrates the active role of consumers as individuals. Complaints and criticism comingle with praise and testimonials. Word of mouth moves at the speed of the Web and reaches far wider than ever imagined. If a customer has something good or bad to say, telling the world beats telling the manufacturer or service provider in a solitary letter. The implications are profound, as a vendor's ability to respond quickly is increasing beyond anything most managers have ever experienced. What organizations still need to build into their operations is the standardization of timely and appropriate vendor responses.

With knowledge, firms identify volatile market needs by coming up with products and services customers want even when the customers don't recognize what they want until it's offered to them. To do this, market leaders need to know deep down what they can offer and what the marketplace will buy. In either direction, seller or buyer—a firm's products and services or customer needs and wants—knowledge is the key.

At the same time, newness is hardly enough. Having something that's different, up-to-date, and even original may win customer attention but it won't keep a business ahead of the pack. That something must make a difference that counts for the customer. It needs to offer enhancement, improvement, ability to do more with less, a convenience or an advantage not previously available, or the capacity to do what was not previously possible. As we demonstrated in Chapter 3, know your customers and they will point the way. Then find the knowledge that will get you there.

In the case of Hartness International, a case-packing manufacturer in Greenville, South Carolina, customers wanted fast (even immediate) service in repairing their machines. The trick was to find out how to provide it. The machines load bottles of soda, ketchup, or beer at high speed and down time is very expensive time. Problems that bring a bottling line to a halt can cost $150 a minute—$216,000 if it takes a technician 24 hours to arrive. Yet on arrival, a technician may take only 10 minutes to make the repair.

Three years after beginning a search in 1995 for a knowledgebased answer to fast repair, Hartness had its customer solution working for more than 50 customer installations in six countries. Repair by video-conferencing became the heart of the solution. The company's technology subsidiary developed a Video Response System (VRS) that draws on the videoconferencing know-how of PictureTel Corp. and uses a wireless camera, remote control, a wireless antenna, and a high-resolution monitor with a second camera on top. VRS enables engineers to direct live, interactive repairs as soon as a malfunction occurs.

An estimated 80 percent of the company's service calls are now handled with a brief, money-saving videoconference.

In a move that epitomizes knowledge transfer, Hartness technicians visiting a plant do more than make repairs. They show a plant's technicians how to fix the machinery, leaving behind know-how for future repairs. For good measure, the technicians leave behind a videotape of the repair session so that plant technicians have a visual record to refer back to. Hartness CEO Bern McPheely aptly calls it "the ultimate form of customer service."[9]

Information Overload. A boomeranging irony at the core of innovation seeking leads to the issue of information overload. In a stunning number of examples, the knowledge a company needs is already vested in the firm but is lost in information overload. Given the volume of information that users and decision makers must cope with, along with the blizzard of electronic communications within firms, information can be a problem as well as the source of a solution.

A Pitney Bowes study documented the problem. The average Fortune 1000 employee receives or sends 178 messages and documents a day. Eighty-four percent of employees are interrupted three or four times per hour by messages; and 71 percent feel overwhelmed by the message traffic. Meredith Fischer, Pitney Bowes' vice president of corporate marketing and chief communications officer, appropriately calls it "a blizzard of communications" that's "beginning to have a seismic effect on people's professional and private lives." The

Gallup Organization, San Jose State University, and the Institute for the Future, which conducted the study for Pitney Bowes, found that new communications tools are not replacements but add-ons to the old familiar ones. Particularly sobering for message beleaguered employees is the finding that 69 percent of the companies surveyed have no guidelines for dealing with communications tools (Figure 4-2). As Fischer states, "Workers are on their own."[10]

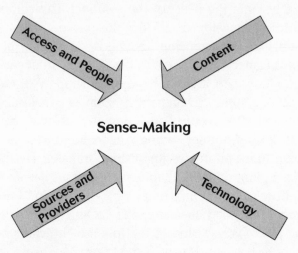

Sense-Making

FIGURE 4-2. INFORMATION OVERLOAD

Overload causes a problem of signal detection—separating relevant "signals" from irrelevant "noise." Left on their own to cope, information recipients are forced to work out their own filtering systems, with varying degrees of efficiency depending on who they are and where they are in the overall information network. What they want are consistent filters to provide uniform and predictable access to information. Duplication of access adds to the overload, as people within a firm send the same message by phone, fax, and e-mail to guarantee that it wins attention and doesn't get lost in the flood of information.

When no protocols exist for communicating information throughout an organization, information does not arrive when and where it is needed. Without protocols for capturing and classifying potentially useful information for retrieval, the company commits time, money, and personnel to gathering what it has already collected. It's common to hear of research projects with relevant findings that become lost in the files. Or worse, they never get filed in the first place, as happened at Ford when its new car developers wanted to replicate the success of the original Taurus design team. No one remembered or recorded what was special and distinctive about the successful effort.[11]

Dealing with the scope, variety, and complexity of computer products creates an information problem of its own. When customers come calling with problems, solutions may encompass hardware, software, and communications components, which are changing nonstop. Never before has it been so imperative for a company to filter the latest information, organize it for efficient retrieval, and make it available for application by service personnel. Hewlett-Packard confronted this challenge with a knowledge management tool, "case-based reasoning," to capture technical support knowledge and make it available globally. There is no mistaking H-P's success in this effort: average call times went down by two-thirds and cost per call dropped 50 percent. In addition, the company now needs fewer technical support agents.

At Hoffman LaRoche, a knowledge management initiative for drug applications provides another example. The firm reformed the complex process of developing voluminous documents for the Federal Food and Drug Administration and European regulatory authorities. The modifications saved the company many months in approval time for several products—at a financial savings of $1 million per day. Such examples crop up increasingly across many industries as awareness spreads about the problem of information overload and the practical benefits of coping with it via knowledge management.

Fundamentally, knowledge management means that managers are not helpless in the face of the changes confronting firms of all sizes, in all industries, and in any market. All firms have the raw material of information, which they then can manage to produce knowledge and profitable outcomes. In other words, there's gold in those mountains of information; but companies need to mine it.

Summary

Knowledge management is not another "silver bullet" that, once fired, solves all business problems in the present and future. Nor is it the latest cure-all theory to sell to management teams that are struggling with their internal problems and the pressures of the marketplace. Seeing knowledge management as a panacea is misleading and misdirected. Instead, look upon it as a realistic response to the world of change and an open-ended process for finding solutions. Fundamentally, it is a hardheaded approach in search of workable strategies. It produces results, which is what doing business is all about. It's a matter of when, where, and how so that firms capitalize on the little-recognized, undervalued, and underutilized asset of knowledge. A company's competitive position depends on how effectively it uses what it knows and how quickly it acquires new knowledge. The challenge is to take action in a fast-changing environment to gain competitive advantage by applying the how-to of knowledge management.

For Further Reading

"Special Issue on Knowledge and the Firm," *California Management Review* 40, No. 3 (Spring 1998).

The entire issue is devoted to seventeen articles by leading experts from around the world on all aspects of knowledge management.

James W. Cortada and John A. Woods, eds., *The Knowledge Management Yearbook 1999-2000* (Boston: Butterworth-Heinemann, 1999).

This is a large, annually published anthology of the best articles and chapters to appear in the previous year on all aspects of knowledge management. It also includes an extensive reference section with information on other publications and Internet sites dealing with knowledge management.

Thomas H. Davenport and Laurence Prusak, *Working Knowledge: How Organizations Manage What They Know* (Boston: Harvard Business School Press, 1997).

Two leading experts describe what knowledge management is within a business environment and how corporations are exploiting it for profit.

Laurence Prusak, ed., *Knowledge in Organizations* (Boston: Butterworth-Heinemann, 1997).

This is a collection of papers on how firms are harnessing and cultivating knowledge for practical business purposes. It includes theoretical, how-to, and case studies.

5

How to Manage
Knowledge

The only irreplaceable capital an organization possesses
is the knowledge and ability of its people. The productivity
of that capital depends on how effectively people share
their competence with those who can use it.
—Andrew Carnegie

*This chapter focuses on the essential components of knowledge
management—content, social capital, and infrastructure—as applied in business and government today. It addresses the problem
of what to do with the enemies of knowledge management and
presents tested principles that take into account the nature of
knowledge and the ways it is generated and shared.*

Hughes Space & Communications, the world's largest manufacturer of communications satellites, wanted to save
time, energy, and money by not "reinventing the wheel"
when its people worked on highly complex, multi-year
projects. So it built an internal "knowledge highway" for employees
throughout the organization.

BP, the giant energy concern, wanted to make certain that the right
source of expertise was brought to bear rapidly on problem solving
and decision making around the world. So it reorganized its global

The lead writers of this chapter are Laurence Prusak and Eric Lesser.

business around the knowledge, processes, and technologies associated with 88 major corporate assets.

Bechtel, the architectural engineering firm, wanted to ensure that its project teams brought to their design decision making all the benefits of discoveries made by other project teams past and present. To do so, it defined and implemented structured knowledge processes.

Whether a firm is building satellites, supplying energy, or carrying out mammoth construction projects, the mandate is the same. These companies, like all others, had to face up to the need to generate and transfer knowledge and improve access to it across the organization. In one way or another, they responded to the imperatives of knowledge management.

While the solutions are distinctive to each organization, the imperatives are universal: What does a firm know? How does it use what it knows? How fast can it know something new and how expeditiously can it make the knowledge available to the entire organization?

Components of Knowledge Management

As Figure 5-1 illustrates, the how-to of managing knowledge has three essential components:

- *Knowledge Content*—What kind of knowledge matters to an enterprise? Where is it found and how is it manifested and demonstrated? How does a firm go about finding and collecting it?
- *Social Impact*—How does a firm foster informal relationships that improve knowledge flow?
- *Infrastructure*—How does a firm provide support and structure for knowledge within the organization? How does it establish and maintain links among people and provide opportunities to create and share knowledge?

This approach is not based on abstract theorems but on the way people do their work. It takes into account the reality that firms are a collection of capabilities and resources with limits on absorptive capacity. What happened in a company's past cannot be ignored. But what counts is not only how the firm builds on what its people already know, but how it puts knowledge to work and creates new

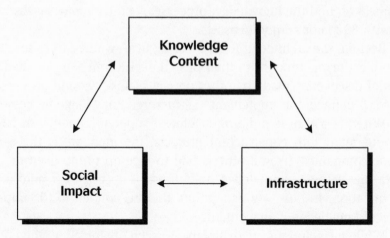

FIGURE 5-1. KNOWLEDGE COMPONENTS

knowledge. Given the fact that firms differ in their knowledge priorities, they must start with their particular business requirements, strategy, and goals in identifying their knowledge resources. In a pharmaceutical firm it can be R&D; in a retailer it can be marketing; in a manufacturer it can be production efficiencies; in a service company it can be response time. Knowing the organization and its business is a prerequisite for identifying what a firm needs to know.

Once this is clear, a firm must identify where its knowledge is located—embedded in databases and documents, embodied in existing business processes, and rooted in employees themselves. Identifying and harvesting these resources is the first step. Who are the employees who span boundaries among functions in understanding how things are done? Who are the knowledge brokers—the people others ask for help in solving problems?

Social capital plays a major role in the way a firm's knowledge gets transferred. It represents the sum total of relationships among people in an organization, thereby providing a context for person-to-person transactions in which the currency is knowledge. In this context, people work together directly without the need for intervening procedures, regulations, and formal structures that can interfere with or slow down the transfer of knowledge. It can be as straightforward as a call across functions to someone with whom the caller shares understanding and trust. Like financial capital, social capital is an asset, no less real because it is social. And it does not lend itself to measurement by standard accounting practices. Unlike financial capital, it is endlessly reusable as along as it is nurtured, maintained, and, ideally, continuously strengthened.

In committing itself to building the social capital needed for effective management of knowledge, management rewrites the informal codes that inhibit knowledge creation, visibility, and dissemination. This involves the care and feeding of connections throughout the organization. The ways to do so include senior management sponsorship of knowledge management initiatives, responsive reward and recognition systems, and employee training and coaching. This basic environmental change redefines what norms and behaviors the company wants and values. Without redefinition, all efforts and investments in processes, organization, and technology by management will be undermined.

At 3M, where pursuit of knowledge goes back a long way, success stories celebrated by the company reinforce the orientation toward the organized use of knowledge by all employees. On its Web site, for example, 3M publicizes the time in 1953 when a laboratory assistant accidentally spilled a fluorochemical liquid coolant on her tennis shoes. No matter how hard she tried to clean the spots they would not go away. Then came the insight: if water couldn't penetrate the spots, then the coolant could become a rain repellent. *Eureka!* Scotchgard™ was born and it now protects clothing, carpets, furniture, wood, and leather. Scotchgard is an excellent example of 3M's innovation-based vision, which requires that 30 percent of annual sales come from products less than four years old.

The firm also cites a 1941 statement by a former president, William L. McKnight: "Mistakes will be made, but if a person is essentially right, the mistakes he or she makes are not as serious in the long run as the mistakes management will make if it is dictatorial and undertakes to tell those under its authority exactly how they must do their job. Management that is destructively critical when mistakes are made kills initiative, and it is essential that we have people with initiative if we are to continue to grow."[1]

Researcher freedom is one of various mechanisms to promote knowledge creation and sharing. The focus shifts from hiding "mistakes" to learning from them by sharing the knowledge the researcher(s) gained. 3Mers can get company research grants and involve other company scientists in their work. Regular meetings and fairs give researchers time and space to share ideas. A Technical Council composed of leaders of the major 3M laboratories meets monthly and goes on an annual retreat to share ideas. A Technical Forum of scientists and technologists holds frequent meetings for knowledge sharing and sponsors an annual three-day knowledge fair. All of this activity is supported by an online database of technological expertise that is accessible across the $14 billion company.

To be effective, a knowledge infrastructure balances processes, structure, and technology and has as its foundation the ultimate source and repository of knowledge: the human mind. Processes collect and disseminate knowledge. Within work processes, a series of steps and guidelines facilitate the flow of knowledge and channel it so that it serves business objectives. Structures exist to direct resources, develop standards, and resolve knowledge conflicts. Technology plays its important role both in collecting and managing explicit knowledge and in serving as a vehicle for people to transfer tacit knowledge.

The U.S. Army, like 3M and other companies, has been well ahead of the curve in developing a knowledge process. Belatedly, its model program for creating and disseminating knowledge has gained the attention it deserves. Founded in 1985, the Center for Army Lessons Learned (CALL) monitors military events, determines lessons learned, and applies them to future operations. CALL members go into the field to observe maneuvers and figure out what soldiers learned. They then feed this knowledge back to unit commanders on a real-time basis.

The Army itself goes even further: it prepares training materials based on the lessons learned. And besides applying what it has learned in real time, the Army also conducts After Action Reviews (AARs) to generate knowledge for use in future operations. The content is military, but as models of knowledge generation, AARs fit any organization. The reviews bring together observers and field personnel to analyze what happened and what was learned. These personnel then identify lessons and operating principles, which are then shared with units throughout the Army.

Whether management is military or civilian, the sharing and spreading of knowledge do not happen without leadership. Management teams that do not seek to establish a supportive environment are going to find knowledge management slow-going and they are likely to be disappointed by the results. Those who succeed establish and maintain conditions that promote the acquisition and sharing of knowledge. At IBM, for example, the management of IBM Global Services has championed the role of Intellectual Capital Management (ICM), the firm's process for creating, sharing, and applying what it learns from client engagements. Consultants are required to give their findings to the ICM database after every project, making the knowledge available throughout the organization. This is in keeping with the goal of making knowledge as widely available as possible, thereby establishing a renewable asset that increases rather than diminishes in value. The more knowledge is used, the better it gets, the more it expands, and the more it benefits both the organization and its people.[2]

Principles of Knowledge Management

When knowledge is embedded in an organization, key principles dominate the landscape. These principles characterize the outlook of the knowledge players in an organization, which at its best includes all levels, all units, and all functions. These principles shape the planning and decision making of management. They also show up in ongoing changes and in improvements in product, process, and production.

True to the interpersonal nature of knowledge exchanges, these principles develop from direct contacts with a wide range of managers who are concerned about and involved in information issues, learning challenges, and knowledge potential. The need to develop these principles was underscored in a research program on new approaches to information management. Executives from 25 major companies, including high-tech leaders in the information revolution, were asked what they needed to know about information. What stood out was an admission that was both humbling and challenging: "We have no real idea how to manage value-added information and knowledge in our companies." The challenge led to an intensive effort to work with a variety of companies and their managements to identify best practices, new ideas, creative responses, and break-throughs in dealing with information. But that was not enough. Broad-based principles for managing knowledge were also needed.

By principles, we don't mean iron-clad commandments or auto-cratic rules. We mean ways of implementing and maintaining effective management of knowledge. Managers who do so are like gourmet chefs. Their menus vary, depending on region, local produce, culture, history and location, individual styles, and price level. Such factors make for and demand variations. There is no one way to run a four-star kitchen. But there are principles to guide the cooking process, and some of these principles are more important than others.

In managing knowledge effectively, the following are important principles that have stood the test of preparation and application:

- Knowledge exists in formal and informal markets within organi-zations.
- Knowledge is not free.
- Technology per se does not change behavior.
- Context is as important as content.
- We learn from one another and through stories.
- Nothing happens without "ground truth" and trust.

Knowledge Exists in Formal and Informal Markets Within Organi-zations. On close inspection, informal networks spring up in organi-zations as "knowledge markets." They develop as employees expand their search for access to knowledge, offer it to others, and broker knowledge within and outside the firm. It is largely an *ad hoc* phe-nomenon in which knowledge buyers and sellers exchange their wares at a fair price. The "price" is typically some form of mutually accepted reciprocity: "I'll help you if you help me in the future." The exchange is real, however rough. The repayment may come directly from the person you help or from someone else who responds to your reputation as a knowledge provider. They help in order to get into the act, figuring that one day you can help them. Payment may also come indirectly: your reputation as a knowledge provider can favorably influence raises and promotions. And let's not overlook the psychological reward of being recognized for what you know as a source of self-fulfillment.

Regardless of management support, knowledge markets grow organically in firms. Individuals who are knowledgeable become highly visible and often receive hundreds of messages per day, testifying to the urgent need for knowledge. Positive feedback encourages knowledge providers to keep up the good work as faster, cheaper, and more easily networked computing facilitates the marketing of knowledge. When people "hoard" what they know and use it to win favor and influence, they take their knowledge out of circulation. When they hide their "mistakes" to avoid penalties or retribution, they deprive the organization of powerful learning opportunities. When organizations do not reward knowledge sharing in their performance measurement and recognition systems, they send the message that it pays to keep knowledge to yourself.

In contrast, knowledge brokers answer questions that make it possible for people to do work faster, better, and more smoothly, and even to perform in new ways. In the course of the day, they may receive messages from people who want to know how something was done in the past, where they can find particular experts, what others have done previously to solve a stubborn problem, and what they themselves can do today. These knowledge brokers might have been there and done it. Or they might function as knowledge "collectors," who learn from the experiences of others by extracting principles and the "rules of the road" that they can use in other situations. What counts is that they can recognize patterns, identify lessons that they and others can apply in new situations, and figure out what principles to put to work. They span boundaries among functions, units, processes, and specialties. They can get out of their box and they are able to think like others. They can turn data and information into knowledge by adding context, meaning, and interpretation. They are the place where knowledge in organizations ultimately exists: within individuals.

Knowledge Is Not Free. In the threefold investment of time, money, and energy in knowledge, time is the scarcest organizational resource. It is also the most easily misunderstood, largely because the engineering model for using time does not apply. Knowledge management is based on a paradox: "wasting" time (standing around talking, chatting informally, exchanging information at the water cooler) is a productive way to develop knowledge. Output does not mathematically match input of time (or money and energy). Instead of *Get back to work and do something,*" the knowledge mantra says, *"Talk about work and learn something."* Hard-pressed as they are to have enough time just to answer their messages, managers glaze over at any suggestion that they *just* hang around and talk. Nonetheless, in organizations where knowledge flourishes, managers will tell you that the investment in time is a necessity if you want to get anywhere with knowledge management.

On the money front, it "costs" to set up facilities so that employees get together face-to-face in on-site lounges or electronically via groupware and videoconferencing. Add to that the cost of "down time," if that is defined as time away from handling daily duties and responsibilities.

As with time and money, energy is also in limited supply. People have only so much energy to pay attention, to engage in exchanges, and to follow up on possibilities, particularly when they see no immediate payoff.

Technology per se Does Not Change Behavior. Tools, in and of themselves, do not make fundamental changes in the way people in an organization interact, communicate, and conduct interchanges. People who send too many memos send too many e-mails. People who fail to make meaningful connections when given information on paper will not do any better with electronically transmitted data. People who do not listen in meetings are no different in chat rooms. Sending messages faster will not make them more significant. Colorful presentations will not transform trivial information into relevant findings. When it comes to knowledge, faster is not necessarily better. And getting "there" does not count so much as recognizing "there" as a destination.

Context Is as Important as Content. Trying to transfer knowledge without providing context is like handing out apples from the "Tree of Knowledge": you hand out the result (an apple), but you say nothing about how the apple was grown or the consequences of eating it.

Transfer of knowledge depends on sharing context so that people can understand the *how* and *what for*. This requires a common "language" that encompasses recognizable concepts, code words, and professional jargon. The more people understand the setting in which knowledge is generated, the greater the chance that they'll be able to replicate the process and apply what's been learned.

In Boston, when a contractor working on the Boston Harbor tunnel project wanted to introduce innovations in the drilling process, the firm followed the standard engineering style of explaining the innovations in memos, manuals, and diagrams. But it got nowhere with the innovations, which had been developed by New Zealand tunnelers used by the contractor. The contractor not only resisted the expense of flying in the tunnelers to explain the innovations; he also reasoned that documentation would do the job. It didn't. Finally, the contractor had to bring together the New Zealand and Boston tunnelers so that in face-to-face discussions, hands-on demonstrations, and socializing over rounds of lager, the New Zealanders could successfully transfer their knowledge.

Make no mistake: Context is the link among data, information, and knowing how to put both into action to produce outcomes. Knowledge is the differentiator and the enabler. The executive summary of a report provides only the results, without involving readers in the process that enables them to apply the same principles and techniques. Where changes are involved (and that's where knowledge is a firm's crucial asset), immersion in context and firsthand experience foster transfer of knowledge. Surgeons don't learn to operate and pilots to fly only by reading manuals and textbooks.

We Learn from One Another and Through Stories. When people make direct, real-time contact with each other, they can transfer knowledge to one another at more levels than they realize. This is particularly obvious when the contact is face to face and an exchange takes place across the verbal and nonverbal range of the intellectual, emotional, visceral, and sensory. Often, the transfer is unpredictable and spontaneous, sometimes innovative and creative, as real-time exchanges draw out of the people ideas, thoughts, and insights of which they weren't aware. These are live, unrehearsed events, highly productive in the management of knowledge. Where face-to-face meetings are not possible, phone calls and videoconferencing are filling the bill, providing many of the benefits of face-to-face contacts in real time. Peter Murray and Andrew Myers of the Cranfield Business School cite evidence of this trend in a survey of European executives: more than 60 percent are using or plan to use some form of video-conferencing technology.[3]

Companies that recognize the value of direct exchanges have set up directories of knowledge providers. At Deere & Co., it's called a "People Who Know" directory. Want to find someone who can answer questions about the company's piston liner kit or coolant filters? Type key words into your computer or phone an 800 number and get the name, qualifications, and phone number of the right person to ask at the tractor maker's technical center. At IBM, an intellectual capital system (usually called an ICM) enables users to call up résumés, identify interests, and pinpoint the individuals responsible for the deliverables in a specific project.

In transferring knowledge, stories go to the heart of the matter. They appeal to mind and heart by conveying knowledge in the most compelling way. They *tell* by *showing*. They provide coherence, explain in the concrete, and show results. They embody knowledge-producing experiences and humanize them. In any exposition of theory, telling a story builds a bridge to practice. In any presentation, the two words *"for example"* are immediate attention-getters.[4]

As the literature on organizational culture emphasizes, people learn about their firms, their jobs, their duties, and their opportunities from the stories they hear. To choose one among the many testimonials on stories, there is the comment of one-time bond salesman Michael Lewis in the best-selling *Liar's Poker*. In recounting his experiences at Salomon Brothers, he calls the firm's training program "without a doubt the finest start to a career on Wall Street" and then labels the training materials "the least significant part of our training." Then he adds: "The relevant bits, the ones I would recall two years later, were the war stories, the passing on of the oral tradition of Salomon Brothers."[5]

Nothing Happens Without "Ground Truth" and Trust. In war and in business, knowledge is tested on the ground, not in an ivory tower. Military personnel who have seen wars lost at headquarters are the first to recognize the consequences of losing sight of this reality. Executives who have seen the best-laid headquarters plans for products and services go awry are not far behind. Listen to what both military personnel and executives call "war stories" and their descriptions of "life in the trenches," and you will hear testimonials to "ground truth," the apt phrase used by the U.S. Army at its Center for Army Lessons Learned.

CALL is a model of knowledge management, from its origins to its implementation. A senior officer who read Tolstoy's *War and Peace* late in his career was struck by the difference between Tolstoy's realistic accounts of Napoleonic War battles and the way they were taught at military academies. Tolstoy had interviewed battle veterans to find out what it was really like on the ground compared with classroom abstractions—the difference between what was supposed to happen and what actually happened. As we already noted, when the Army conducts after-action reviews at the center, it pursues "ground truth" by calling together both enlisted soldiers and officers to discuss what each knew and how and why they made decisions.

The road to knowledge is paved with such realities, but only if there is trust all along the way and at all levels. The trust must be visible to the members of the organization, who should be able to plainly see how the firm credits and rewards knowledge providers and sharers. When the firm singles out knowledge providers and sharers for recognition in knowledge directories, and when these employees stand out on promotion lists, the message comes across. At the same time, when the company rewards knowledge hoarders (as many do), the message is undermined. Since trust tends to flow downward, members of top management must lead the way in sharing with each other as well as the rest of the organization.

Enemies of Knowledge Management

In observing or participating in more than 100 knowledge projects over the past five years, we have encountered 101 ways—if not more—in which knowledge management can be at risk. This is understandable, not only because systematic attention to the subject is relatively new, but because knowledge itself, as described in Chapter 4, is intangible, fluid, process-oriented, and difficult to quantify. These characteristics notwithstanding, it is particularly important to detect errors about knowledge management so that it doesn't become yet another management fad that promises much but delivers little.[6]

Of all the errors that put knowledge management at risk, there is a root error that contributes directly to all others: resistance to distinguishing between data and information on the one hand and knowledge on the other—and, more important, the resistance to dealing with the implications and significance of this fundamental difference.

Resistance is understandable. The education of managers has not oriented them toward knowledge in the way it has been set forth in this chapter and the previous one. By training and experience, managers are fact- and information-oriented. They see themselves as traveling at full speed on the "Information Highway" en route to what has been proclaimed by many pundits as the "Information Revolution." Managers aren't geared to the deep-seated reflection and understanding that the concept of knowledge requires, nor do they typically consider the hurdle of investing the requisite time, money, and energy.

In addition, there is the distraction of popular management literature that dismisses the difference between data/information and knowledge. This literature argues that dealing with the distinction distracts managers from managing effectively. The argument has had its effects, intensified by a suspicion that comes from viewing knowledge management as yet another panacea—in a long list stretching back to the 1960s.

Within organizations, many executives cite an anti-knowledge attitude that forces them to do knowledge work by stealth. Such executives make comments like: "We had to disguise our knowledge project within a data warehousing architecture plan." Resistance persists, despite the factors that cry out for exploiting knowledge in response to what is happening in the marketplace, in technology, in the global economy, and in the competitive environment of today and tomorrow.

To protect knowledge management from both friend and foe, here are some glaring errors that manifest themselves as enemies of knowledge:

Knowledge Stock Is Emphasized to the Detriment of Knowledge Flow. When knowledge is not differentiated from information, it is defined in terms of stock rather than flow. It is seen as a thing or an object that can be captured, transmitted among individuals, and stored in a variety of ways. This is a view that persists in the way organizations think about knowledge. But it misses the point about knowledge, which is in constant flux and change and is central to day-to-day doing and operating by, for, and of individuals. Knowledge is not *out there*; it is in people who develop it, transmit it, and leverage it. Knowledge doesn't pile up; it flows.

Knowledge Is Mistakenly Viewed as Outside the Minds of Individuals. The proper way to view and handle knowledge is in terms of knowers. Although one can represent, and often embed, knowledge in organizational processes, routines, and networks (sometimes in document repositories), it cannot truly originate outside the minds of individuals. Never complete outside people, knowledge is shaped by one's initial stock of knowledge and produced by individual reasoning applied to new data and information.

Yet managers and their staffs persist in viewing knowledge as having a life of its own. They dub databases "knowledge bases," view search engines as if they were human brains, and talk of executive expert systems as if the human mind were incidental to their construction and use. Such ongoing attempts to dress up old technologies in new "knowledge" labeling persist as serious obstacles facing knowledge advocates.

Tacit Knowledge Is Neglected. Management must recognize the importance of tacit knowledge and deal with it as a screen through which explicit knowledge is captured, assimilated, created, and disseminated. Neglect it and you undermine the leveraging of knowledge. The central role of tacit knowledge is based on what it entails: a body of perspectives, assumptions, perceptions, beliefs, and values. As such, it can dominate the way managers view data and information and, more important, what they do with it in order to create knowledge and produce outcomes.

When managers ignore tacit knowledge, they can fail to learn from data and information. They prejudge, make assumptions, and dismiss what they should take into account. The history of corporate follies is proof enough. In an example that will resonate among mid-level managers, there is the case of the firm that commissioned a customer survey to identify its strongest selling points. Management was convinced that service was the firm's greatest appeal. But that conclusion didn't emerge in the survey's findings, which placed service as no better than fifth or sixth in influencing purchases. What happened? Management rejected the findings of the customer survey when the survey contradicted management's assumptions.

Failure to Connect Knowledge and Decision Making. A fundamental tenet in managing knowledge is that it is inseparable from thinking and action—that is, decision-making. When individuals process data and information in order to know something of importance to the firm, they don't create knowledge for knowledge's sake. It is not an end in itself, as happens too often with knowledge initiatives. In effective management, knowledge is the fruit of discussion, dialogue, and discovery of what's significant as the basis for making decisions and taking action.

Ignoring the Future, Focusing on the Past and Present. While firms *"cannot know the future,"* they ignore it at their own peril. Every strategy, decision, and action is somehow related to future expectations and outcomes. Knowledge management is so powerful because it has the ability to create shared context in order for an organization's members to address rewarding opportunities in the future. Knowledge is managed so that a firm can examine change, view the ways the future is emerging, identify how the future might unfold, and, most important, focus on the implications for decision making and action.

What Can Management Do?

To go beyond raising their own awareness about the enemies of knowledge, managers can address ways and means of overcoming these enemies and moving their organizations toward becoming more knowledge-driven. To do so, three closely related imperatives emerge from analyzing knowledge management in a variety of firms.

First, a firm, led by its top management, must continually reflect on knowledge as an organizational phenomenon and develop a consensus about knowledge itself. This is especially important because the implications of knowledge, both for individual behavior and decision making by any employee, are typically not self-evident. They must be developed, however, by management. Specifically, here are some action guidelines for managers to follow:

- Develop shared understanding at local levels, since knowledge tends to be a local phenomenon (e.g., within an office, department, or organization).
- Allow individuals rich and frequent opportunities to discuss and debate what knowledge is.
- Help individuals identify their current and desired knowledge roles.
- Ask individuals to identify knowledge implications for group behavior and processes.

Second, managers must be obsessive about identifying and correcting errors in their own body of knowledge—or, more precisely, in what they *think* they know. This is necessary because knowledge, as we have already emphasized, must be seen in terms of flow; it is in continuous need of updating, checking, and rechecking.

Here are some questions to ask about any issue or topic, from products to services, from customer relations to developing new markets:

- What do we know or think we know about the different aspects under consideration?
- Have we identified our own perceptions, beliefs, assumptions, and projections?
- How do what we know and what we do not know affect specific decisions by an individual?
- What do we need to know and how is it different from what we think we know?
- What errors must we watch for? How might they affect our decisions? How might we avoid these errors?

Third, managers must monitor themselves and their organizations. They must be vigilant in order to detect and correct errors in the processes of knowing—all the ways in which knowledge is generated, exchanged, and leveraged throughout the firm. Here are some action-oriented questions that management must confront:

- Which individuals play what roles in creating, sharing, and reusing knowledge?
- Which individuals or categories of individuals are not involved in dialogue around specific issues and topics? How might their involvement contribute to the content and flow of knowledge?
- How do the organization's structure and systems facilitate or impede knowledge flow?
- How does tacit knowledge influence the generation and transfer of explicit knowledge?
- How is technology used to unearth and influence tacit knowledge?
- What role do experiments play in knowledge generation?

Summary

The imperatives of knowledge management are future-oriented for a basic reason: When knowledge stands still, it limits an organization to the past and present and ignores what lies ahead. Any organization in which knowledge stagnates places itself in jeopardy by cutting off connections to its future. Companies facing this type of situation tend to adapt a passive rather than proactive role in the marketplace.

In pinpointing the significance of knowledge, IBM's chairman and CEO, Lou Gerstner, makes a compelling prediction: "I believe that future leadership companies and future leadership institutions of all kinds will be those that know how to compete and win on the basis of knowledge—learning, adapting, and improving the use of this vital asset."[7] In this context, competencies enable organizations to leverage knowledge as venture capital that can carry them successfully into a future filled with change and an unavoidable degree of uncertainty.

For Further Reading

Kuan-Tsae Huang, "Capitalizing on Intellectual Assets," *IBM Systems Journal*, 37, no. 4 (1998), pp. 570-583.

Describes IBM's Intellectual Capital System (ICNM) and lessons for other firms implementing an ICM.

Kuan-Tsae Huang, Yang W. Lee, and Richard Y. Yang, *Quality Information and Knowledge* (Upper Saddle River, NY: Prentice Hall 1999).

This is a tactician's guide to the development of Information Capital Systems and processes.

Harvard Business Review on Knowledge Management (Boston: Harvard Business School Press, 1998).

A worthwhile compendium of knowledge-related articles published in the *Harvard Business Review*.

Liam Fahey and Robert M. Randall, eds., *Learning from the Future* (New York: John Wiley & Sons, 1998).

An interesting collection of essays on the use of scenarios to build organizational knowledge.

Janine Nahapiet and Sumantra Ghoshal, "Social Capital, Intellectual Capital and the Organizational Advantage," *Academy of Management Review*, Vol. 3, No. 2 (1998), pp. 242-266.

An article highlighting the importance of social capital in the knowledge management arena.

Etienne Wenger, *Communities of Practice: Learning, Meaning and Identity* (Cambridge: Cambridge University Press, 1998).

An insightful text by one of the leading thinkers in the area of communities of practice.

6

The Leveraging of Knowledge

There is no knowledge
that is not power.
—Ralph Waldo Emerson

This chapter describes the role of competencies in contributing to a firm's success: how to recognize them, put them into action, and benefit from them. The chapter also reviews specific cases of competencies at work.

On March 27, 1997, a once-endangered motorcycle company celebrated the tenth anniversary of becoming America's first Japanese luxury import marque. Only eight years after putting its Acura car on the market with 60 dealers, it had reached one million sales. On the tenth anniversary, it had 270 car dealers selling its car of distinction and also had, for good measure, a line of outboard motors featuring 50 different models and variations.

This now familiar Honda story is a parable of the difference knowledge can make when a firm identifies a competency and puts it into play in the marketplace. The company had come out of World War II in competitive trouble as a Japanese motorcycle maker with dim prospects, but with one thing going for it: the ability to build effi-

The lead writer of this chapter is Scott H. Oldach.

cient engines at low cost. Over the years, the company had perfected this ability to the point where it was ahead of everyone else. When management decided to leverage low-cost engines into products other than motorcycles, a new competitive force emerged. So in the 1950s, Honda started building car engines and outsourcing virtually everything else that goes into a car. By the 1970s, Honda was mounting a serious challenge to U.S. automobile manufacturers, with a focus on its "trademark" engines, standardized features, and premium prices. From there, the company road led to the tenth-anniversary luxury Acura and to the line of outboard motors.

Canon took a different route in head-to-head competition with Xerox, which at the time owned the market for photocopying. You didn't *photocopy* something—you *Xeroxed* it. Canon came up against a company that had the technical know-how, the resources, and the reputation. Canon even leased much of its technology from Xerox, which had such a stronghold on the market that it could act toward its customers as a *de facto* monopoly. This was Xerox's Achilles heel: high-handed service. So along came Canon's lower prices and a competitive challenge built on superior service. From there, Canon went on to joint ventures and new products, thereby becoming a successful company with varied technologies and a competitive edge in distribution channels.

For Honda and Canon, knowledge leveled the playing field. It gave these companies the power to compete effectively. Both companies began with limited resources in competition with strongly entrenched players. Both companies focused resources around a knowledge-based competency to succeed against firms with superior resources. As we've discussed earlier in this book, knowledge emerges from data and information that are put to work, first by individuals and then by groups to become the wealth of organizations. Unlike other resources, knowledge appreciates rather than depreciates with use; but like all capital, you must use it in order to produce value.

Competencies put knowledge to work. They emerge from the explicit management of knowledge that occurs when a company identifies relevance of its collections of knowledge to the marketplace, organizes and focuses resources, and pursues a customer-oriented, results-based strategy. That's how organizations leverage knowledge.

When identified and mobilized, competencies are logical groupings of resources (human, physical, technical, and intellectual), skills, technology, and processes that differentiate the organization in the marketplace and provide competitive value. They create a framework for a group to think and work together in a positive way to produce results for the organization. This framework holds a group together around a common vocabulary and a way of thinking about the marketplace. A community emerges and benefits from the accumulated experiences of all its members. Its body of knowledge is ready for leveraging.

If a community properly defines a competency around an activity that has value in the marketplace, then the community can continuously pursue its work knowing that each participant will reinforce the group's experiences. Specifically, much of what the community knows is tacit knowledge and remains so. The knowledge is exercised each day through judgments that anyone in the community can apply, without explicit procedures, guidelines, or even rules of thumb. This knowledge emerges through experience. Over time, the competency may be codified into training material or procedure manuals to accelerate the assimilation of new members, but the coin of the realm is experience.

In this context, competency is not limited to skills as traditionally defined by the human resources community. It is much more. A competency embraces procedures, technology, experiences, and marketplace image as well as skills. In addition, the community acts as an informal screen to ensure that each member subscribes to the group's beliefs. In contrast, HR focuses on the question, *"How can skills be defined, developed, and allocated?"*

Typically, the tasks resulting from the answer to this question are performed by individuals or by a "skill class." While this approach can provide an engineering-like efficiency, it easily overlooks tacit knowledge and the different ways the organization imparts and leverages knowledge in the marketplace. It readily identifies "hard" skills that are formalized, like accounting and engineering, but it tends to neglect the importance of informal skills, like evaluating the sound and smell of a machine during operation—what we identified as tacit knowledge in Chapters 4 and 5. Formal skills are only the tangible tip of the competency iceberg.

The information technology community has come along with another version of competence dominated by software. Starting with the developers of expert systems about a decade ago, IT has applied technology in a variety of ways either to supplement or to displace human understanding. Learning systems, expert systems, and now collaborative systems all stem from a common focus on process software. These tools facilitate the formalization and sharing of knowledge by developing modeling mechanisms. The models force groups to examine tacit knowledge and, often, to unfreeze knowledge, but they do not create tacit knowledge or leverage knowledge to create new opportunities. They take the gold coins out of the proverbial mattress, count them, and make them available for withdrawal, but they don't enable the coins to grow in value.

How to Identify Competencies

Competencies constitute an aggressive approach toward knowledge as venture capital. They are a way to invest aggressively once they are identified, organized, and aligned with each other in terms of objectives and tasks to be performed

The IBM Consulting Group—like any firm can do—rationalized its competencies by starting with its own history. The Group entered the consulting business with a series of services: business transformation, continuous flow manufacturing, supply-chain management, process reengineering, and IT strategy. Each service had its own methodology, its own training, and its own sense of what it was. Each also had its own structure and own set of people, who at times bid against each other for the same projects and clients.

To end the Balkanization of IBM Consulting, the services were called together by the senior executives of the organization and they raised competency-seeking questions: *What is the essence of your knowledge? What distinguishes it? Who values it? How is the knowledge formalized, and how is it transmitted? How do you put it to work for the organization?* Essentially, IBM Consulting examined what it did with clients in a structured set of workshops to uncover its competencies. Beginning with the types of engagements (a consulting firm's equivalent of products), each group delineated the key value it delivered. The IBM Consulting Group's various practices did this by examining standard processes to uncover where knowledge was essential in delivering on engagements. In addition, experts were assembled by senior management and asked to identify other experts.

Together, these activities resulted in an initial list of potential competencies. Each competency (knowledge, process, experience, and tools) was then modeled by consultants expert in the subject areas. During the modeling, when it became evident that many competencies overlapped, they were collapsed into one competency. The remaining competencies were verified against customer evaluations to determine whether customers recognized their value and to ensure that the competency was unique when compared with what the competition offered. Finally, the competencies assembled their intellectual capital into a blueprint showing how competencies relate to each other to present a value proposition for the Group's customers. In the end, IBM identified six basic abilities in its consulting organization:

- *Customer Value Management*—the ability to understand how the Group generates value among customers and to differentiate between customer wants and needs. This competency includes the ability to link knowledge of customers to a firm's specific processes that satisfy or dissatisfy its customers, that make a difference or fail to make a difference in attracting them (the subject of Chapter 3).

- *Competitive Focus*—the ability to understand how a firm competes and therefore how it should focus its resources to strengthen its competitive position. The firm can link this knowledge to both processes and technologies so that the firm aligns its competitive advantages with day-to-day operations.

- *Process Engineering*—the ability to model a firm so that end-to-end activities and functions support customer needs. The model is then analyzed by potential users of the model to figure out how to improve the activities that support customers and to identify the optimal skills required of the people involved in these activities. Also included is the ability to simulate complex processes to determine how they can be best managed on an ongoing basis.

- *Architecture*—the ability to identify, analyze, and group similar markets, products, and channels to create both an industry and a business blueprint. This extends to the applications, hardware, and networks a firm needs to align its technology and business resources.

- *Emerging Technology Assimilation*—the ability to identify and relate uses of new technologies so that they provide value for the organization. This includes forecasting how the firm can assimilate new technologies and identifying both barriers and facilitators of assimilation.

- *Organizational Change*—the ability to design an organization in support of strategic goals and to prepare a transition plan to transform an organization from its current model to a new model in an orderly manner.

Next, we searched for tangible signs of knowledge as an asset that we have and that we can share with clients. This is not to say that a company can codify and count all knowledge like figures in a profit-and-loss statement when, in fact, most knowledge can't be quantified this way. But a conscious effort to identify what we know and how we know it goes a long way toward making the knowledge available throughout the organization. This becomes a powerful way to raise consciousness about knowledge as a major asset in every organization.

In the IBM Consulting Group, the hunt for tangible signs of knowledge encompassed such obvious indicators of staff output as books and articles, white papers and reports, speeches, procedures and methods, and tools. Word of mouth and the grapevine made contributions as well. Each competency collected and categorized its own knowledge, which facilitated the formation of the community and the emergence of a shared knowledge framework.

We then formed networks and communities based on competency. These networks and communities were knowledge bases that became rallying points for specialists and experts within the consulting group. They also presented a way to attract people from outside the company. Inside the company, people were forming meaningful clusters to which others were added from the outside.

Each competency manages its own core of knowledge and its corps of experts, who are free to develop their own view of the marketplace and to respond to the needs of particular clients. The top people in each group meet regularly so that they get to know each other. They share experiences and compare problems and solutions. They form a community that carries on knowledge exchange in informal contacts—from brief exchanges on the phone to discussions over lunch and in all-day conferences.

In developing a knowledge-based competency, each group formalized its base of knowledge to the degree possible and appropriate. The groups began by collecting existing components of knowledge and organizing them into a shared mind map of the targeted knowledge. In doing so, the groups found that gaps and overlaps emerged. The gaps became development targets. The overlaps opened up new insights by highlighting different approaches. Practitioners also made requests of the competencies in order to develop their own knowledge base. If they had recurring needs, they could contract with the competency networks on a formal basis and budget accordingly for participation.[1]

Why, then, didn't IBM merge all of its competency centers into one grand center? For the same reason a firm shouldn't merge all of its competencies into one overall Kremlin of power and control. A competency in marketing should not be forced into a merger with a competency in manufacturing. People with skills in these areas can and must work together, but the community must keep its eye on the particular goal without getting caught up in territorial struggles and issues of control and power.

Within the context of learning and knowledge, what counts is not who's in charge, but who knows what and how does it apply to the needs of the client or firm. Within the IBM Consulting Group, a debate went on that parallels debates on knowledge management in all organizations. Should there be a "configurator" who matches people, problems, and goals? Or should the "configurator" be a method embedded in a computer? Who assembles the people with knowledge and mobilizes them so that they apply the competency in the most effective way? The answer, in a consulting group, is the individual responsible for solving the problem. At IBM Consulting, for example, a managing principal as chief problem solver is responsible for understanding the context of a problem and assembling the appropriate human and technological resources to resolve any issues the problem presents. In a company, it is the individual given responsibility for the competency and for putting it to work to produce competitive advantage. The governing principle is clear: one individual does not and cannot know it all, but the person in charge must know where to go to find out.

For example, one client approached IBM wanting to combine knowledge of the consumer marketplace with technology to improve shareholder knowledge. The client assumed that Lotus was the complete answer. But once the managing principal analyzed the problem, it became clear that Lotus was merely a *component* of the solution, not the *entire* solution. Our knowledge of Lotus and Lotus Notes implementation became part of a solution that involved knowledge management, process engineering, architecture, and competitive focus. What emerged was a customized engagement that combined formalized competencies with emerging competencies (knowledge management, in this case) and products to meet the client's specific need.

While companies may not have the luxury of customizing every response in dealing with a business issue, service, or product, leveraging knowledge is particularly significant in new product innovation. Honda did this with its engine competency. The company went beyond limiting itself to specific engines that already existed and explored ways to modify engines to fit new contexts. Such flexibility can lead to creative solutions without increasing product risk. At some companies, new product development consortia take advantage of existing competencies throughout the organization. Boeing, for instance, with its 777 design, drew on its competencies in aircraft manufacturing, component manufacturing, aircraft operations, and aircraft maintenance.

How to Benefit from Competencies

The great value of competencies is that they create a context for learning and stimulate experimentation. They are a natural habitat for what Tom Peters has identified as organizational "fighter pilots," individual learners who find meaning in experience and find ways to apply that meaning. While flying in formation when necessary and ostensibly operating by the numbers, they create value on their own. They learn and put that learning to work for the sake of the organization.

Such is the case with commercial underwriters in an insurance company. They continuously make decisions on risk and premiums and over time they can make or break an insurance company. The "fighter pilots" among them meet informally to discuss risks and compare notes. They may identify a particular group of businesses that can be a lucrative and little-used source of revenue—something like bars, which insurance companies see as a high risk and therefore subject to higher premiums. Three or four underwriters may support each other in writing special business for bars. The informal network they create can be the beginning of a competency and a profitable line of business.

"Fighter pilots" turn up wherever there is work to be done and tasks to be completed. One of them turned up unexpectedly as a taxi driver in Paris at rush hour on a Friday. I was racing from a meeting to catch a plane in 45 minutes and was warned that it was at least a one-hour trip at that time of day. Faced with the prospect of missing the plane and then waiting several hours for the next one, I told the driver what I was up against and asked him to get me there on time. He realized immediately that a bonus (a larger-than-normal tip) was part of the deal. The driver drew on his knowledge of traffic patterns at that time of day, of the least-congested on- and off-ramps, and of shortcuts. Off he went, roaring through the back streets of Paris and, when appropriate, using the expressways. It was a virtuoso driving effort that got me to the airport on time and earned him a tip that doubled the fare.

You might view this experience as a Gallic anecdote worth telling over a few drinks or as an example of the birth of a competency at a cab company. What does the cab driver know that can be put into action? He knows his city map, which anyone can master by studying it. He also knows the traffic rules and conditions and how they vary depending on the time of day, the weather, the season, and so forth. Again, anyone can know that. In the United States, where traffic reporting is a radio mania, drivers can hear about the latest conditions, though not always in time to do them much good. For taxi drivers, there are also on-the-road reports from fellow drivers, typically relayed via taxi dispatchers, not to mention the benefits of news reports about major accidents, parades, or the arrival of dignitaries and their traffic-jamming motorcades.

All of this is still not enough to develop a competency with a marketplace advantage. Jumping to a technological solution with a database and formalized input is not the answer, even if you pay for knowledge contributions. Paying for knowledge often buys bad or unusable knowledge, as too often happens with R&D units. They come up with great research and findings, but there is a difference (and a disconnect) between new knowledge and putting it into play. Often, the knowledge is used by *other* companies to create products *they* can sell. This happens for any number of reasons: the knowledge went unrecognized because it wasn't encouraged by company culture, it violated the accepted wisdom of the firm, it was crushed by office politics, it seemed to threaten the firm's main line of business, or it lacked advocates. For whatever reason, the new knowledge went nowhere.

As for our Paris cab company, there is no incentive for individual cab drivers who are caught in a traffic jam to share the information, because they are already stuck. They must see the long-term self-interest in doing so, which they'll recognize over time as other drivers' information offers benefits to them as their collective pool of knowledge grows. These cab drivers become part of a community built on shared benefits and interests, from which a sense of camaraderie emerges independent of a formal structure.

When it's at work, a learning ecology is incredibly productive at no extra cost. Learning becomes sharing, sharing becomes learning, and it spreads. People are drawn into the community as knowledge seekers directly recruit others. A desire to be included builds on concern about "being left out." A sense of belonging holds the community together and results become so absorbed into the learning process that metrics cannot keep up with them. When a cab driver is in the habit of contacting his dispatcher or another driver to check on whether all is clear at a particular expressway merge, he is engaging in a learning transaction. But don't tell him that! It just makes sense to him. That's just what he and his fellow drivers do.

Cab drivers engage in a higher level of learning when they experiment and store the results in their memory. This is what my Paris cab driver did to get me to the airport on time—saving the crucial 15 minutes. Faced with traffic jams and rush-hour traffic in the past, he experimented. And from those experiments, he learned how to beat the averages. He developed an internalized database, and so have other experimenters in the cab company.

The company does not have a competency so long as its drivers keep what they know to themselves. It is up to management to capture what its experimenters have learned and to facilitate sharing. What experimenters learn carries different weight depending on the business. In this case, the cab company's competency is its reliability and its ability to beat the clock in delivering customers to their destinations. Management's job is to collect and codify the relevant traffic knowledge, part of it standard (traffic patterns, routes, regulations), part of it the fruit of experimentation and experience (the source of a competency advantage).

Management can turn to the grapevine and to the informed scouting reports of its managers (in a cab company, dispatchers) to identity the experimenters who are its "fighter pilots." They are typically the "go to" people in an organization, known to informal networks. They turn up as people sought after for committees and projects for change. Inspection of operating and productivity data helps in finding them. At the taxicab company, they are the drivers generating the highest revenues, thereby delivering extra value every hour they're behind the wheel. In manufacturing, you'll find them in units that have the lowest rate of rejects and the highest production. In R&D, they are units most successful in developing knowledge that leads to marketable products.

The knowledge equation is not complete without customers. (Here, Customer Value Management comes into play.) Not only would customer reactions (by filling out response cards) help the cab company in identifying experimenters, but customers could also participate in experiments to find the best routes to avoid traffic problems at congested times of day. The customer in this case becomes an unpaid "consultant," a bridge between R&D (looking for the best routes) and marketing (what customers want and will pay for). Now the cab company is on the way to codifying knowledge for a competency that offers the competitive edge of on-time service and more: faster service. Given the time of day, destination, and starting point, the taxi company can offer the fastest possible trips—at a premium that enough customers are ready to pay.

In this light, competency becomes a bridge between what a firm has to offer and what customers will buy. Factoring in the customer is the way to identify competencies that deliver a payoff. Such was the case with S.C. Johnson & Son, Inc., (Johnson's Wax) in the 1950s, when it lived up to the intention of Chairman and CEO Sam Johnson: "We are not managing the company for the next quarter. We are building for the next generation." The answer in the 1950s was aerosol. The firm put it in wax, recognizing it had the making of a wide-ranging competency. From that point on, the firm leveraged the knowledge it had acquired. It added aerosol to air fresheners and hair sprays, creating a portfolio of products, and then expanded into the over-the-counter drug market.

This is not to say that competencies come with a no-risk guarantee of competitive advantage. A number of ingredients are required to ensure the effective deployment of competencies: a clear understanding of what you know and how it relates to the resources of the firm, matching marketplace opportunities to capabilities and knowledge domains, and identifying and reaching the customers who will respond to the product/service and appreciate its value.

This raises a chicken-and-egg question over whether a competency is embedded in a process or a process is embedded in a competency. The authors of this book view competencies from the perspective of knowledge and that they encompass process as well as people and technology. If processes were viewed as independent entities, they would end up driving strategy from too restricted a viewpoint. In fact, competencies may call for coordinating two or more processes in order to deliver results in the marketplace.

Such coordination worked to the benefit of two companies writing auto insurance for selected groups, USAA (officers of the U.S. Armed Services) and Progressive (high-risk customers). Since profitability depends on the ratio of premiums to claims paid, these firms needed to link high or low loss frequencies with their targeted groups of customers. This requires knowledge derived from two processes, underwriting and claims, although typical process modeling separates them as different and does not synchronize them. The actuaries at these companies make the difference by bringing together knowledge from both sources to develop the insights they need to set profit-generating premiums and to develop underwriting guidelines.

The more we examine competencies, the clearer it becomes that they are the ways and means of keeping up with and adjusting to change. Paradoxically, knowledge-based competencies resemble the medieval craft world in the flexibility they provide, with today's added dimension of scale made possible by technology. Command-and-control systems do not work in this setting. They can destroy the shared set of purpose, the commitment of individuals to group efforts, and the exchange of knowledge by pushing people to look to the top for solutions. By contrast, competency-oriented players look to *each other* for solutions.

Consider what must happen in a firm with a knowledge-based competency in miniaturization. To capitalize on the competency, management needs to lead the search for ways to create value by applying miniaturization to products and services—in a new context and a new environment for a new result. Limiting a competency to one product trivializes it and throws away its power. The other way of trivializing a competency is to let the participants in the process become generalists instead of focusing on their knowledge core. At full force, competencies push firms to seek out, recognize, and apply multiple ways to expand their power to compete successfully, whether in efficient engines, aerosol, or miniaturization.

Putting Competencies to Work

In enabling companies to get the most out of competencies, IBM Global Services has confirmed time and again the importance of an advocate, particularly in avoiding the pitfalls in putting competencies to work. An advocate is the individual, usually an executive, who funds, supports, protects, and nurtures the development and use of a competency. A successful product or service needs an advocate so that it will continue to flourish by capitalizing on its underlying competency. Advocates already exist as brand or product managers. A second type of advocate is new: the advocate of the competency and the promoter of new applications in as many ways as possible. Both the new and old advocates follow roads that lead away and then back to a competency, and it is up to management to recognize a competency as both starting and end point.

High-level support for competencies is particularly urgent in American companies, given the fact that competencies are a recent development in management thinking and planning in the United States. In contrast, circumstances and national culture provided a fertile ground for competency thinking in Japan, where the nation had to rebuild after World War II. Japanese firms, short on financial and physical resources, put a premium on human capital. As a result, competency developed naturally, strengthened by the strong sense of national identity and the cultural emphasis on sharing and consensus.

In the give-and-take of firms and in the world of mergers and acquisitions, advocacy for competencies has twists and turns. Part of the complication arises when competencies are in competition for company resources or when one competency is chosen over another. At one plant run by Oscar Mayer in Madison, Wisconsin, the plant manager, when asked what his plant did best, did not respond by saying "meat products." Packaging was his answer. His people had great skill in figuring out how to put ten hot dogs or five pounds of ham or three pounds of turkey together. "We do the best packaging in the industry," he boasted. The company recognized the competency and turned to the plant in deciding, for instance, whether to sell a particular item in six-or eight-unit packages.

When Kraft bought Oscar Mayer, the word went out to plant managers to reorganize their plants to be flexible enough to turn out a range of products—ham, hot dogs, cheese, cookies. Manufacturing flexibility was the competency the new ownership focused on as it faced a fluctuating marketplace that was almost impossible to predict. Oscar Mayer offered manufacturing capacity, and it offered a brand name. As for competency in packaging, Kraft did not place a premium on it. Instead, Kraft pursued efficient distribution strategies around dry, refrigerated, and frozen products. In making a decision on allocating resources, Kraft set aside the packaging competency.

At times, a company can overlook the value of an old competency and assume that it's time for a change. This is a compelling phenomenon in the technology area, where nothing in the marketplace gets so old so quickly as last month's model. Newness for its own sake is as American as the nearest auto showroom or electronic store, where the latest product gleams and beckons.

The phenomenon of moving to something new happened at a financial company that decided to discard an old technology—transaction control program (TCP)—in favor of COBOL, and to convert its TCP programmers to COBOL. Management overlooked the strong marketplace demand for TCP programming, which it could profitably supply with TCP competency. It would have made sense to hold onto and market the TCP competency while developing COBOL competency separately. Notwithstanding, although the company considered this distinctive strategy, it went ahead with the expensive retooling and migration.

Now that competency thinking is maturing in the United States, in East Asia, and, increasingly, in Western Europe, companies can apply a tough-minded, well-tested approach to competency, step by step:

- *Identify* the fundamental components of your organization's knowledge that can be valued by both customers and service providers. Quantify the value using market research. The components you identify become your building blocks.
- *Model* the competencies in terms of processes, technologies, skills, and content along four dimensions:
  - shifting knowledge from tacit to explicit—in effect, doing an inventory;
  - deploying knowledge so that the organization knows where it is and how to get at it, creating a "directory" that facilitates retrievability;
  - identifying the value the firm's knowledge can create for customers; and
  - pinpointing how that knowledge differs from what other firms offer—the basis for competitive advantage.
- *Architect* competencies to products, both tangible products and intangible products (services). Competencies are not inherently saleable. They don't fly off the shelf with a price tag attached. They are a component of what a firm can offer customers. So it is necessary to deploy people with the right knowledge and in the right combination to make a competency work as part of a competitive product.
- *Leverage* by searching for different contexts and different environments for applying the competencies. Take a *what if* view of

the marketplace. Start with what customers want and/or need. Then look for ways the competency can make current products and services more competitive and, most rewarding, look for completely different products and services.

Focus on creating a blueprint showing how products and services interrelate to serve customer needs. This is a *back-and-forth* view of the various pieces of th blueprint that identifies not only what services should be, but also the ways a product needs to be enhanced in the first place, when it is designed and produced. Eventually, firms will be able to configure competencies as sub-assemblies, dynamically creating unique customer solutions that deepen the firm's relationships with customers. The firm will then be able to capture the knowledge of this customer experience and use it to design a better product—on and on.

Summary

With competency-based strategy as a driving force, firms use their knowledge as venture capital. Knowledge "finances" aggressive investments, not merely to keep up with the competition, but to get ahead and to aim at domination of the company's markets. Knowledge management has emerged as one of the most effective new strategies of the 1990s, particularly for companies that want to add new products and services or are experiencing growth in sales, market share, and complexity of operations. Because competencies do not thrive in a vacuum, a holistic approach must bring together the various parts of a company so that they operate in sync with strategy.

Between managing knowledge and putting it to work to achieve results, there is a gap to be filled with process-centric management— the focus of the next two chapters.

For Further Reading

Debra M. Amidon, *Information Strategy for the Knowledge Economy* (Boston: Butterworth-Heinemann, 1997).

This is a convenient introduction to the use of knowledge in business.

Nicolai J. Foss and Christian Knudsen (eds.), *Towards a Competence Theory of the Firm* (London: Routledge, 1996).

This is an excellent introduction to the application of competencies within a firm. It includes research, cases, and frameworks.

Laurence Prusak (ed.), *Knowledge in Organizations* (Boston: Butterworth-Heinemann, 1997).

A series of articles by various authors that presents applications of knowledge and competency-based strategies.

James Brian Quinn, *Intelligent Enterprise: A Knowledge and Service Based Paradigm for Industry* (New York: Free Press, 1992).

This is the book that introduced many managers to how competencies could help grow a business. It remains "must" reading.

Gary Hamel and A. Heene, *Competence-Based Competition* (New York: John Wiley & Sons, 1994).

For nearly a decade, this book has been the bible on competencies, based on business patterns of the 1980s and early 1990s. It is an excellent introduction to the topic.

Part Three

MANAGING BY PROCESS

7

The "X" Factor in Transformation

Processes are not magic,
but they can have magical effects.
—Michael Hammer

While organizations can put in place procedures and projects to become process-centric, a culture is often missing. We identify this as the "X" factor in transformation, whereby all the parts and people in an organization operate in alignment to deliver value to customers. This chapter describes how this alignment occurs. It also discusses the role processes play in overriding the silo effect of functional boundaries and in establishing connections across an enterprise. As demonstrated by best practices in process management, a holistic approach that changes company culture relies on three key ingredients: coordination, cooperation, and communication. As implementers, process leaders mobilize company resources and deploy them to specific goals. What then emerges is process-centric management.

Traditionally, when executives from sales, manufacturing, finance, information technology, human resources, and customer service gather to discuss transformation of their company, they talk, respectively, about change in terms of

The lead writer of this chapter is Thomas S. Hargraves.

sales, manufacturing, finance, information technology, human resources, and customer service. They look at the company through the windows of their own departments or disciplines. Function dictates outlook and input and, eventually, shapes operations.

What is missing is the "X" factor in transformation—the process mindset that encompasses the totality of what all employees do and their interconnectedness in terms of creating value for customers and results for the company. Our point of departure is that in today's changing marketplace, every firm must be process-oriented. The most effective companies already are. As the operational nucleus of a core competency, process is neither a choice nor a preference, but a necessity. *At its core, process is a group of tasks and activities that are brought together to create value for customers.*

To address transformation, change, and process meaningfully, a holistic outlook views the company in terms of how it operates, how its various parts contribute to the totality of the enterprise, how day-to-day activities fit together, and, most important, how it all responds to customers. A company's entire management team must think in terms of clustering activities into processes that are joined together to meet customer demands. To do so, managers must understand customers and markets, their wants and needs, and the products and services that meet those wants and needs. Process is nothing less than organizing activities in the most efficient, effective way to produce the optimal result for the customer—and thereby pay off for the company and its shareholders.

Internally, process-centric management unleashes the power and resources of the company, as all its units and the people in them see themselves as interconnected and work that way. This is evident not only in the way company business gets done, but in how individual managers make decisions. The head of production, when faced with a decision on adjustments in a new line, factors in the effect on pricing. A company lawyer dealing with a copyright issue considers marketing implications. The CIO selecting a software application makes the choice in terms of business strategy and company goals.

Externally, process-centric management positions a company to respond to change whenever and wherever it arises and to take forward-looking steps ahead of the competition. Most important, it establishes a business improvement strategy with answers and actions that respond to the fundamental marketplace question: *Where do our customers want us to be and how do we get there?*

With such an approach, a company develops a customer-defined vision of what is an ideal delivery of value (as set forth in Chapter 3). The customer becomes the ultimate driver of processes and the overall mission of the company is defined in terms of serving customer needs and wants. Process is not a function, such as finance, engineering, or sales, which in and of themselves (and as necessary as they are in the firm) don't deliver value to the customer. In the course of everyday operations, functions are task-based and their functionaries can become task-obsessed, absorbed in performing the work at hand without reference to the larger picture. When faced with problems outside their area, these employees have a familiar refrain: *"That's not my job."* However disguised, this (spoken or unspoken) response translates into sub-par performance.

Team sports provide an obvious analogy. Star players pay off in results only when their talents are harnessed to a team effort, augmented by the appropriate combination of supporting talent (resources), fueled by the right chemistry (team spirit), and led by a coach (process leader) with the appropriate strategy. Individual skills (like functions) are blended into the process of playing together. In sports or in business, stars may win games—but teams win championships.

Shifting from function to process changes a firm's philosophy and culture. The enterprise, rather than the organization, becomes paramount, as structure no longer gets in the way of getting the job done. A cross-functional approach replaces a functional focus with a process-centric view. Faced with a need for solutions and decisions, sales talks to billing, marketing talks to manufacturing, distribution talks to R&D. And the change goes even further: the process of developing products replaces the function of R&D, order fulfillment replaces logistics, obtaining orders replaces sales. There is no denying that functions do the work, but it is processes that achieve profit-generating goals.

Instead of a group of people pursuing similar activities (in a function), a group of people work toward a common goal as part of a process. Whereas an organization's efforts and activities were once fragmented, they become integrated. Instead of measures that are inner-directed and that run the risk of self-delusion, measures are turned outward toward the real-world test of customer response. Management does not settle for self-congratulations without validation from the customer and the marketplace—nor does it want to.

As processes deliver value that counts in the form of products and services for customers, they become the connective tissue of a company, organized and linked together to produce marketplace results. This is not to say that functions are abolished, for they are necessary for the maintenance of any organization. They are how and where work is performed. What emerges is a *matrix organization*, since it is unrealistic to think of functions as expendable, however invisible they are to customers. As with a four-star restaurant, customers do not see (or want to see) the cook prepare the meal. They come to consume and enjoy what's on the menu.

Where processes are in motion, they all must be interconnected and linked to each other and to all other processes in the organization. The resulting matrix structure applies a process mindset and a holistic approach. We know today that where matrix organizations have failed, project managers (as they were called) failed to provide strong leadership. Process leaders (as they are called today) succeed when they have clear lines of responsibility and authority so that they can overcome silos and deal with goal conflicts. They do not abolish functions. They coexist with and complement the firm's functional units by cutting across boundaries that interfere with the goals of processes. Functions, in turn, are not limited to one process.[1]

The Three C's of Process

In clustering activities in the most efficient, effective way to produce optimal results for the customer, a process organizes people and resources without prejudgments and without departmental or functional restraints. In this framework, a process-centric organization means a high degree of involvement and full-scale participation at all levels. Management leads the way in creating a culture of process by absorbing, inculcating, and applying *the three C's of process: coordination, cooperation, and communication.*

At its best, business success resembles a World Cup victory in soccer. Everything comes together after a season of coordinated effort in which all the players on the team subordinate their functional efforts to the ultimate goal. They work together to win games (make sales) by satisfying fans (customers) with victories over the competition (superior products and/or services). The players see themselves as fitting in as part of a joint effort under the strategic direction of their manager (CEO). The result shows up in winning the World Cup (becoming No. 1 over the competition).

Coordination doesn't rely on hunches and educated guesses, but on well-founded answers to questions based on strategic goals, company assets, competitive advantages, and changing market conditions. The answers, which are aligned to customer values, guide management in bringing together working parts to establish processes aimed at results. To do so, management unfreezes the structure of the organization and reassembles its parts. In future projections of what organizations will be like, they have been described as operating in a "fluid" or virtual state, resembling Legos or process blocks that can be connected or unconnected as required. A basic rationale is at work: the marketplace is continuously changing. Processes enable firms to continue transforming in order to keep up.

Cooperation, which is everyone's job, must become contagious. Management must reject the acronyms of resistance: INMJ ("It's not my job"), IDWIT ("I do what I'm told"), IDMB ("I did my best"). They must replace these acronyms with WAITT ("We're all in this together"), which puts a premium on exchanging resources, solving problems jointly, and making decisions in a participatory style—in other words, creating *high-performance teams*. A culture of sharing emerges as people discover resources they never knew were there and benefit from contributions that come from every unit in an organization, including units seldom heard from.

Communication moves data, information, and knowledge throughout an organization so that employees can put it to work. Successful firms establish a continuous system of knowledge exchange in an open, sharing, and flexible atmosphere (a key theme of Chapters 4 and 5). Access to relevant information must match the information needs of the players; facilities to exchange information must be readily available. In the end, the premier medium is people, each of them an expanding "database," a problem solver, and a reservoir of personal "software" drawn from individual thinking, training, and experience.

Communication tools, applications, and solutions are at management's disposal—from groupware to videoconferencing, from quality management practices to process reengineering. The challenge for management is to align the organization around processes and their goals, reinvent their enterprises, and establish a system for the free and smooth flow of information and knowledge. When this is done well, what emerges is an organization that unleashes its power and resources, as all of its parts and people see themselves as connected and work that way. This is evident not only when processes are set in motion, but in how decisions are made by individuals, teams, and even committees—in concert.

To facilitate communication, firms are looking to information technology to support the dissemination and sharing of data, information, and knowledge. These enterprises employ the latest innovations as enablers. (Chapters 9 and 10 on technology will pursue this topic in detail.) For example, some companies are employing data-mining techniques to improve processes aimed at customer intimacy. In handling information, firms are using techniques such as bio-infomatics to analyze data so that it becomes useful for new product development. In the area of knowledge, techniques like groupware, collaborative sharing, and Lotus Notes are being used across R&D, manufacturing design, and new product development. The stakes increase exponentially with e-business, which relies on access to information throughout an organization to facilitate process performance. By the very early 2000s, business-to-business e-commerce revenues are projected to reach $268 billion, a clear sign of the opportunities on the immediate horizon.[2]

Process-centric management positions a company to respond to change and opportunities whenever and wherever they arise, and to take forward-moving steps ahead of the competition. Most important, a process mindset establishes a business improvement strategy with answers and actions that respond to the fundamental marketplace question: *Where do our customers want us to be and how do we get there?* With such an approach, a firm establishes a customer-defined vision of delivering value. The customer drives the firm's processes and its overall mission, with results measured in present and future success in the marketplace.

In many successful examples—such as GTE, Coca-Cola, IBM, GE, and ABB—firms have established processes and created linkages among various areas of their business. They represent an emerging trend in process-centric organizations as they tackle issues such as linking process and information technology requirements and coordinating investments made in both. This has led to the establishment of process IT units. IBM, for its purposes, has combined the process leader and the IT owner so that decisions and investments meet the requirements of both. The stakes call for such linkage. As greater amounts of money are being invested in IT, with implementation taking place over longer periods of time, misalignment between IT and process or strategy can involve costly mistakes. That's why firms are creating a single organization that has responsibility for both business process and IT decisions.

Questions and Issues

In action, the process mindset raises and addresses questions like these:

- *What are the most important parts of a firm's operations in terms of strategic goals?* In analyzing their competitive landscape, managements must make critical decisions on where to direct the organization. These strategic choices often dictate changes in investment priorities, focus, and deployment of resources. Processes are the levers that make it possible to deliver on these choices.

- *What are the crucial links?* For management, the imperatives center on customer intimacy, supply-chain management, and product-to-market efforts. None of these can be approached in isolation. They are elements to combine and couple and, if appropriate, to separate and uncouple. For example, a supply-chain management process encompasses manufacturing plants, order fulfillment, and distribution, all coordinated in terms of meeting customer needs.

- *What can firms appropriately outsource?* Traditionally, companies have made decisions on outsourcing in terms of specific functions, such as information technology, accounting, or payroll. In recent years, business process outsourcing, which makes sense for some organizations, has become more common. With process thinking, outsourcing decisions depend on which processes are most effectively and efficiently performed within the firm and which are best performed outside the firm. This depends on the strengths and know-how of the firm. A basic management principle applies: do yourself what you do best and draw on others for what they can do better in terms of efficiency, cost, and resources. At the same time, also expand your firm's knowledge of those areas that are crucial to its long-term success.

- *What are the key processes that deliver on a firm's competitive advantages?* While key processes differ from one company to another, even from one subsidiary or division to another within a company, all managements face the same challenge: capitalizing on their strengths as differentiators and sources of competitive edge. Each management team must identify its crucial levers, much like a baseball pitcher with a specific (and limited) assortment of pitches and a great number of variables to deal with in facing his competition (a lineup of batters). A company must figure out the right choices and the right sequence of choices (the right processes). A pitcher facing a batter has a choice of which pitches to throw and when, taking into account the individual batter, the batter's strengths and weaknesses, his recent performance, whether he is left- or right-handed, the presence of base runners, the inning, the condition of his arm, the layout of the outfield fences, and the score. Decisions, decisions, decisions in the face of countless variables and limited options!

Company variables range from demographic trends to the latest technology, from the fluctuating price of materials to transportation costs, from the state of the dollar to the level of inventory. And always there is the competition, from the local to the global. Management must factor in the company's capabilities, potential, and resources and decide how to mobilize them. Process-based responses provide answers that work.

Overall, an evolutionary pattern has developed since the late 1980s in identifying key processes. With the advent of reengineering and the openness to change, firms focused on back-office processes, like purchasing, in order to identify the benefits to be gained in time and money. As companies became more comfortable with processes, they turned to front-office activities that related to customers, such as order fulfillment, and then to commerce-based processes, such as order acquisition and confirmation. Increasingly, firms are focusing on differentiators and developing processes for new product development that are integrated with customer needs and wants. In moving the boundaries from inside the company to outside, firms are transforming themselves and even the marketplace in applying process management. They're also weaving knowledge management practices into these processes.[3]

High-Level Processes

By identifying and focusing on high-level enterprise processes, firms can achieve better understanding of their operations. In doing so, they will recognize that they already have processes at work in their organizations. Without processes in some shape or form, they would never get products or services to market and would never serve their customers. But typically, processes remain fragmented, buried, and/or invisible. They develop over time on an *ad hoc* basis, with varying degrees of efficiency (or inefficiency). Largely unsupervised, they become a patchwork of coalitions, arrangements, exchanges, and all the other ways people get their work done as they see fit: a phone call here, an occasional meeting there, last-minute cooperation, accidental solutions, crisis-driven responses.

When processes develop haphazardly, a turf syndrome develops over time. *Ad hoc* processes can stand in the way of setting up well-planned, effective processes that involve the entire organization. Boundaries are drawn, walls built, "Keep Out" signs posted. This is where change management consultants have been in particular demand—to change a company's mindset in favor of coordination, cooperation, and communication.

A high-level view enables management to take control of processes and get the most out of them, a need that in the late 1990s became widely recognized. In fact, this is the basis of the Process Classification Framework developed by the International Benchmarking Clearinghouse of the American Productivity & Quality Center (APQC).[4] "The intent," as APQC states, "has been to create a high-level, generic enterprise model that will encourage businesses and other organizations to see their activities from a cross-industry process viewpoint instead of a narrow functional viewpoint." Many organizations already have used the Framework to understand their processes better, APQC reports. As a comprehensive inventory of processes, the Framework is invaluable as a starting point in developing a process-centric approach to management.

Different processes have different degrees of relevance, depending on the individual firm and its particular context. But in our experience, there are three processes stand out as crucial for all firms.

1. Understanding and Managing Markets and Customers. Customer management has the three dominant elements of identification, measurement, and monitoring. To *identify* customer needs and wants, firms rely on qualitative and quantitative assessments, ranging from customer interviews and focus groups to surveys. *Measurement* involves assessing satisfaction with products and services, complaint resolution, and communication. The *monitoring* dimension covers both changes in the market and customer expectations by spotting any weaknesses in product/service offerings, matching innovations with customer appeal, and tracking customer reactions to what the competition offers. At IBM, for example, a process labeled Customer Relationship Management (CRM) encompasses the totality of customer and market needs. All business activities involving customers are coordinated by a single process owner across all of IBM worldwide. After taking ten years to mature, CRM continues to evolve in response to market realities.

2. Producing and Delivering (Supply-Chain Management/Order Fulfillment). Parallel processes apply to manufacturing-oriented and service-oriented organizations, taking into account their differences while affirming their similarities in producing value for customers and results for the organization. In most organizations, these issues and resulting activities come under the heading of order fulfillment or sup-ply-chain management to ensure that customer orders are processed efficiently and effectively. To do so, the firm coordinates forecasts, planning activities, inventory, logistics, and delivery capabilities.

For manufacturing-oriented organizations, a *plan-convert-deliver-manage* process is at work to meet customer specifications and require-ments. First, a firm *plans* for and acquires necessary resources, which is a combination of signing up the best suppliers, purchasing capital goods and materials, and acquiring the right technology. Second, the firm *con-verts* resources or inputs into products, setting up and scheduling pro-duction, moving materials and resources, and making, packaging, and storing the product. Third, *delivery* involves shipment, installation, and arrangement for servicing. Fourth, the firm *manages* the production and delivery process by overseeing order status, tracking inventories, main-taining product quality, performing maintenance, and monitoring envi-ronmental constraints.

For service-oriented organizations, a *plan-develop-deliver-ensure* process is at work. A firm *plans* for and acquires the resources it needs by selecting and certifying suppliers, purchasing materials and sup-plies, and installing the appropriate technology. It *develops* human resources skills by defining skills requirements, implementing appro-priate training programs, and managing skill development. To *deliver* service, the firm identifies each customer's requirements and the resources needed to meet them, then provides what's needed. Finally, the firm *ensures* quality of service by monitoring results.

3. Designing Products and Services. The process of developing new products and services is an ongoing response to the pressures of continuous change. Firms have no choice, as Hewlett-Packard Chair-man and CEO Lew Platt has said so succinctly: "Whatever made you successful in the past won't in the future." Firms have a nonstop requirement to anticipate customer needs and wants and translate them into products and/or services. Whether the focus is on enhanc-ing current offerings or developing new ones, the targets involve quality, cost, life cycle, and timing, supported by the latest technolo-gy. Along the way, products and services that present problems must be improved or replaced. Most firms are looking toward this macro-process as the way to differentiate themselves from the competition.

It is where their competitive intelligence and corporate secrets reside and it is the way firms integrate market requirements with new product development. The goal is not differentiation, but uniqueness.

The journey begins with prototypes—their design, building, and evaluation. This involves specifications, concurrent engineering, value engineering, and patent applications where appropriate. Once prototypes pass the test of effectiveness and customer value, the next stage of designing and testing production of a product gets under way. Down the road, the customer, as judge and jury, is waiting to deliver the marketplace verdict with the decision to buy or not to buy.

Each of these processes requires major commitments of company time, attention, and resources in its own right. Each is necessary to the success of process-centric management. Each is needed in organizations that want to transform themselves successfully in the current environment and to compete effectively. We can't stress it enough: success depends on implementation of these processes.

Depending on the firm, the industry, and the marketplace conditions, other processes come to the fore and become focal points. Even a summary look at each of them highlights how complicated and extensive they are. We could write a book on each process to show how each extends beyond functions to organization-wide goals and marketplace outcomes.

Additional Processes to Implement

In addition to the major processes specified above as necessary in all process-centric organizations, there are some others to consider from the APQC inventory.

Developing Vision and Strategy. Monitor the business environment by analyzing the competition; identifying economic trends, political factors, and regulatory issues; and taking into account demographics, social and cultural changes, and ecological concerns. Then define business concepts and organizational strategy by selecting relevant markers, developing a long-term vision, formulating a business strategy, and developing an overall mission statement. Finally, design the organizational structure and the relationships among units and set organizational goals.

Marketing and Selling. Market products and services to relevant customer segments by identifying those segments and their needs. Develop marketing messages that communicate benefits and back up the messages with pricing and advertising strategies. Respond to orders and enter them into the production and delivery process.

Invoicing and Servicing Customers. Develop, deliver, and maintain customer billing with an invoice and response system. Provide after-sales service, a system for handling warranties and claims, and a system for responding to information requests and customer complaints.

Developing and Managing Human Resources. This is a demanding process with many issues: creating and managing HR strategies, bringing strategies to the ground level of work, deploying personnel efficiently, developing and training employees, supervising performance, rewarding and recognizing employees, ensuring employees' well-being and satisfaction, maintaining employee involvement, handling labor-management relations, and developing human resources information systems.

Managing Information Resources. After developing information plans and tactics based on business strategies, establish and deploy enterprise support systems. Also, implement security systems and controls, direct information storage and retrieval, facilities and information services. Facilitate information sharing and communication.

Managing Financial and Physical Resources. From budget development to capital planning, the process encompasses resource allocation, finance and accounting, report information, tax issues, and facilities management.

Executing Environmental Management Programs. Formulate environmental strategy, ensure compliance with regulations, train and educate employees, direct remediation, and implement emergency-response programs. In addition, the process should include strategies for managing government and public relations, supporting and implementing information systems, and monitoring of the environmental programs.

Managing External Relationships. The company must address various audiences—specifically shareholders, government officials, lenders, the board of directors, and community groups. In many ways, this task parallels customer targeting, and it calls for matching skills, strategies, and resources to particular audiences.

Managing Improvement and Change. Once the firm has measured organizational performance (quality, cost, cycle time, productivity), it can make quality assessments in terms of both external and internal criteria and benchmarks. The firm improves processes and systems and implements quality management.

In all firms, whatever processes are in play, they must be linked to each other and to all other processes in the organization. This is what it means for a process-centric organization to transform itself. Its approach is always holistic, evolutionary, and continuous. When large, complex organizations develop a matrix structure to do more with less, a process mindset and a holistic approach enable the matrix to succeed. That's why, for example, IBM could generate at the end of the 1990s nearly 50 percent more revenues with 25 percent fewer employees than it had a decade earlier.

Leading with Process Management

Firms can use high-level processes to create a blueprint addressing the fundamental questions about what a company does, how it does it, and for which customers. This blueprint is a map of what's important to the company, a modeling exercise that articulates strategy in a visual format. Like architects who can "see" a building by looking at a blueprint and identify what needs to be done (and corrected), process-oriented managers and consultants can examine a process framework and identify the important strategy decisions upon which to act.

What counts are the linkages and interdependencies among these processes. This approach replaces the function-focused thinking of Frederick W. Taylor and the Industrial Age. Accountants worked only with accountants, engineers with engineers, salespeople with salespeople—and the production people were off on their own in plants. The result was an organization composed of silos, each doing its own thing. Each then would throw what it was doing over the wall to another unit. If companies were saddled with redundant operations and non-value-added costs, the costs (once upon a time) could be absorbed into a higher price and passed along to the customer.

In the fast-changing times of a technology-driven economy, the walls come tumbling down. Many degrees of separation and isolation of functions in an organization are wasteful and expensive, not to mention unnecessary. They threaten company survival in the globalized marketplace, where *cost, price, flexibility,* and *efficiency* quickly separate winners from losers. Functions, skills, disciplines, and regions must be coordinated—not on paper or with corporate rhetoric, but in action, as is the case with process-centric management.

IBM's handling of order fulfillment exemplified a process-centric approach in the face of a familiar business scenario: a changing environment of customer mix and market fragmentation. The company was in danger of falling behind competitively; its problem was not lack of resources but lack of effective implementation. What had to go was a functional way of operating that kept resources apart instead of together.

With process thinking, fulfillment is treated as much more than simply receiving and fulfilling orders. It encompasses development and design, the making of a product, the product's significant features, its price, its competitive position, and its marketing. IBM proceeded to mobilize the appropriate skills and resources to cover all of these bases with process-based coordination.

Many roads lead to coordination, depending on how management brings the parts of a company together and how management achieves and maintains linkage. For coordination to go forward from the planning stage to continuous implementation, cooperation becomes contagious—the opposite of what happens when separation, isolation, and internal competition become entrenched. The negative scenario is familiar. Over time, the different parts of an organization become "dis-incented" to work together as manufacturing stays away from sales, marketing eyes public relations suspiciously, and finance steers clear of legal. In making decisions, executives focus on short-term financial or divisional objectives rather than on longer-term customer and corporate goals. In managing, they focus on getting ahead, not on getting the company's work done. Playing the company game counts for more than getting results. People square off to protect territory. Functions become island fortresses.

Process thinking promotes the opposite atmosphere—a spirit of cooperation—by taking down "Unwelcome" signs and fostering an open-door mentality. The operating premise that "we're all in this together" places a premium on joint problem solving, participatory decision making, and collective action. It creates a culture of sharing. And it unearths resources and fosters contributions from every part of the organization.[5]

New Forms of Leadership

Watch for new forms of leadership and managing to emerge in process-centric organizations. Executive management teams will still lead the way but—as already is evident—with an open style that crosses and mixes functions and creates new combinations of skills and duties. In particular, the effective process leader emerges as the one responsible for harnessing resources and know-how to get results from processes. What's new about the process leader is not the skills required to manage, but the distinctive combination of skills and traits that are most important. Such process leaders:

- listen—and learn by listening,
- recognize and work with disagreements that stem from differences in roles and specialties,
- know how to delegate while also staying on top of a process in motion, and
- view people as individuals who have skills to contribute and are able to work comfortably with all functions.

In 1993, Michael Hammer and James Champy drew a job profile that identified the challenges process leaders face. Given the responsibilities, a process leader "should be a senior-level manager, usually with line responsibility, who carries prestige, credibility, and clout within the company.... [They] are usually individuals who manage one of the functions involved in the process that will undergo reengineering. To do their reengineering jobs, they have to have the respect of their peers and a stomach for reengineering—they must be people who are comfortable with change, tolerant of ambiguity, and serene in adversity." Besides clearing hurdles within the organization, process leaders "motivate, inspire, and advise their teams" while acting as "critic, spokesperson, monitor, and liaison."[6] In sum, process leaders have a formidable job profile that reflects the importance and difficulties of leading a process.

Top management in process-centric firms supports process leaders by spreading process thinking, first by example and then by encouraging and rewarding it throughout the company. It takes leadership of a new and special kind—leadership that stimulates others at every level—to lead the firm in whatever directions are appropriate and possible. Participatory management, which is widely accepted, has built a foundation for a next stage of management: collaborative leadership.

The dean of American leadership studies, Warren Bennis, has newly explored the theme of collaboration under the guideline that "none of us is as smart as all of us." He emphasizes that "collaboration is not simply desirable, it is inevitable" in a global economy in which timely information is "the most important commodity." Bennis cites an instructive survey of senior executives of international firms. Korn-Ferry, the world's largest executive search firm, joined with *The Economist* and asked who will have the most influence on their global organizations in the next ten years. Sixty-one percent responded "teams of leaders," compared with only 14 percent who said "one leader." "In these creative alliances," Bennis notes, "the leader and the team are able to achieve something together that neither could achieve alone. The leader finds greatness in the group. And he or she helps the members find it in themselves."[7]

In our view, collaboration emerges when the three C's of process prevail: coordination, cooperation, and communication. At all levels of an organization, process-centric thinking frees individuals to see beyond their individual jobs and duties and to discover leadership potential. It opens them up to new knowledge, prompts them to spot connections they otherwise might have missed, and gives them a sense of empowerment that comes from recognizing where they fit into the overall operation and how they can make a difference.

The more knowledge is shared in an organization, the greater its benefits. The more it is used throughout a company, the more value it delivers. The more it is shared, the more likely it will lead to new formulations that produce new knowledge and new solutions. The greater the input from different individuals with their different portfolios of knowledge, expertise, skill, experiences, and thinking styles, the better the odds in favor of coming up with optimum solutions and the less likely that crucial variables will be overlooked.

Firms learned in the 1990s how important it is to establish a continuous system of knowledge exchange in an open, sharing, and flexible atmosphere. Access to relevant information and knowledge must match the needs of the participants; facilities to exchange information must be readily available. Collaborative technology already is here: groupware, videoconferencing, Internet, Intranet, and Extranet. But companies are still learning to put the technology to work.

In an exploration of how technology can link people in an organization, James L. Creighton and James W. R. Adams looked for ways in which companies made conscious efforts to build and maintain collaboration systems. The researchers found beginnings and innovations, but "no single company" that uses all the approaches that Creighton and Adams describe. They found people who think about meeting rooms and how to conduct effective meetings, information technology departments that are active in setting up connectivity, and people who foster teamwork and collaboration. "But nobody is in charge," the researchers report. "There is no corporate strategy to improve collaboration organization-wide."[8]

In fostering and maintaining communication, people constitute the premier medium as "database," problem solver, and reservoir of thinking, training, and experience. Most important, each individual in a company provides the best kind of connectivity: face-to-face contact. If the traditional meeting of executives from sales, manufacturing, finance, information technology, human resources, and customer service were reconvened in a process-centric environment, functions would fade into the background (though certainly not disappear) as processes dominated in the foreground. Participants would emphasize process performance by problem solving and redesign. A new perspective and a new vocabulary would dominate the discussion as the emphasis shifted from "what we do" to "what gets done." The participants would understand how their work contributes to a larger process and the big picture. Instead of individual inputs, the participants would reach for outputs.

In such a meeting—and in all of a firm's activities and operations—the "X" factor of transformation will dominate: a process mindset that encompasses the totality of what all employees do and their interconnectedness in terms of outcomes for the firm. IBM sees this happening already with its clients. In such an organization, look for process-centric management to take over a firm's decision making, its use of resources, and the way it operates at all levels. In this way, firms will meet the challenges of today and tomorrow and respond to cascading change by putting process-centric management into action.

Summary

No matter how much management tools and techniques change, firms need a process approach and discipline in the present and in the increasingly unpredictable future. A process mindset builds in change readiness and establishes flexibility as an ongoing ability to respond to new demands, pressures, and opportunities. In the context of the fast pace of change, information technology has shortened cycles drastically and enabled firms to be in a continuous state of readiness. The three C's of process—coordination, cooperation, and communication—have become a prescription for responding to new situations, creating a clear mandate to master the implementation of process-centric management. How that's done is the subject of the next chapter.

For Further Reading

Bjørn Andersen, *Business Process Improvement Toolbox* (Milwaukee: ASQ Press, 1999).

While there are many how-to process design books, this is one of the better practical guides, reflecting best practices in evidence at the end of the 1990s.

Ron Ashkensas, David Ulrich, Todd Jicks, and Steve Kerr, *The Boundaryless Organization* (San Francisco: Jossey-Bass, 1998)

This book is full of strategies for managing across functional borders in a process-centric fashion.

Howard Gardner, *Leading Minds: An Anatomy of Leadership* (New York: Basic Books, 1995).

As with process management, books on leadership abound. This is one of the best, with many case studies that help set a context for the leadership style we propose.

James F. Moore, *The Death of Competition* (New York: HarperBusiness, 1996).

The author sets forth the impact of integrated approaches upon work and the marketplace.

James M. Utterback, *Mastering the Dynamics of Innovation* (Boston: Harvard Business School Press, 1994).

This is a book filled with historical and contemporary cases of "doing it the right way."

Process Management in Action

Institutionalization of process management requires
the peaceful coexistence of the vertical and
horizontal dimensions of an organization.
—Geary Rummler and Alan Brache

This chapter describes what happens when firms move toward
process-centric management and transform the way they do
business. These companies position themselves to respond to
change with an organization-wide approach that pulls together
functions, resources, and know-how. The hallmark is flexibility.
The focus is the customer. The outcome is competitive leader-
ship that keeps pace with a changing marketplace.

At a firm with long-standing market leadership, a customer
crisis was building up. Customers were complaining, distributors were criticizing operations, and employees were
grumbling. The ABC Company (note: the ABC Company
is a composite example based on actual consulting experience and
results, but presented anonymously to respect client confidentiality)
had prided itself on a reputation for marketing and distribution excellence as a major source of its competitive edge. But the firm was
beginning to hear a different message, which a company executive

The lead writer of this chapter is Thomas S. Hargraves.

summed up as follows: "Although our competition is not that great in meeting customer expectations, we are hearing disturbing reports about our own dealings with customers. The way our system is now operating, we are getting a reputation as tough to do business with."

The company's sales force was aggressively selling special pricing, and its account managers were responsible for alerting the retail sales force at least 90 days in advance so it could sell in sufficient volume to cover advertising and display costs. However, promotional plans were often not fixed until 45 days in advance. Even on that tight schedule, communication to sales reps was sporadic. On top of that, many members of the sales force were not keeping accurate sales records. As a result, the company was experiencing extensive out-of-stock problems.

Customer complaints, echoed by distributors and employees, called for a portfolio of improvements:

- clearer pricing and greater agreement among all parties,
- earlier communication in pricing so that customers could take advantage of market opportunities,
- reduced duplication in contacts and paperwork (invoices, statements, pay points, etc.),
- greater order flexibility, and
- improved responsiveness and execution.

The firm's operations—characteristically—had evolved over a number of years to deal with tactical and immediate needs. It was an *ad hoc*, here-and-now approach that developed in response to problems and situations as they arose. Various units went their own way in terms of tasks to be performed and jobs to be done. The operation failed to address issues like user-friendliness, technological updating, and adequate integration with business strategy. On the one hand, the firm failed to promote empowerment; on the other, it did not control operations.

As happens typically with all firms, signs of trouble in the marketplace made management take notice. The firm risked alienating and losing major customers, who expected the company to live up to its past reputation for excellence in marketing and distribution. The competition added to the threat with the potential of dramatically improving its order fulfillment and thereby gaining a market edge. Internally, ABC management realized that the firm was failing to capitalize on opportunities to empower its workforce and improve efficiency by eliminating costly redundancies, excess bureaucracy, and ineffective control mechanisms.

A process redesign scenario for order fulfillment epitomizes a response at ABC Company that mirrors what has been done in any number of firms that have undergone transformation. The shift is from emphasizing the logistics of *taking* orders to *fulfilling* them in terms of customer needs and wants. Instead of using measurements that are *internal*, the company develops *external* measurements in terms of the customer. Instead of people doing similar activities individually, a team of people work toward a common goal collectively by performing various activities. An integrated operation replaces a fragmented system.

The following improvements are based on actual cases in comparing the results of shifting from functional to process-centric management:

- Standard order cycle—reduced from 30-40 days to 10 days.
- Premium order cycle—from 10-13 days to 1-5 days.
- Custom order cycle—from 40-50 days to 23 days.
- Production cycle—from 8-15 days to less than 3 days.
- Submittal cycle—from 3-5 weeks to 5 minutes.
- Inventory turns—from 8 to 20.
- Sales—from $108 million to $159 million.

Transformation Drivers

In the marketplace, where firms are spread across the functional/process continuum, process redesign must take into account the distinctive characteristics that set individual firms apart from each other. Typically, functional organizations are commodity-based, characterized by a slow customer-to-market evolution, co-location, and mass production. They are dominated by the standard functions of sales, manufacturing, finance, information technology, human resources, and customer services. At the other end of the continuum, process-centric organizations are characterized by solution design, solution delivery, and after-sales support. Goals of individual functions play second fiddle to customer-based results.

Typically, before transformation, firms lean toward either function or process. Where function prevails, we routinely observe that disparate goals and measures encourage uncoordinated operations. People resist change, particularly if they can point to results as measured by their functional silos. When they ask, "If it's not broken, why fix it?" they fail to recognize what meaningful "fixing" involves. A unit that is working on its own terms may not only be operating far below its potential, but may also damage the organization as a whole—regardless of how productive it looks in terms of its own narrowly based measurements.

In those instances where isolated processes happen to work well, the participants tend to resist integration with newly developed processes. They may regard themselves as "experts" in process, who see no need to involve themselves in other processes that they see as getting in their way. Paradoxically, such organizations can be more difficult to transform than function-centric organizations because the participants create deviant, individualistic versions of their roles (Figure 8-1).

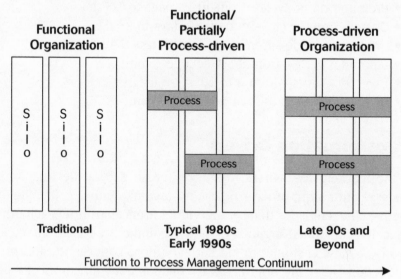

FIGURE 8-1. FUNCTION TO PROCESS MANAGEMENT CONTINUUM

No matter where firms are located in the functional/process continuum, two main drivers—vision and operations—move them toward process redesign and transformation. The best-laid plans begin by identifying which driver dominates and then taking both into account in designing processes. Otherwise, projects will be compromised, even thwarted, when the firm changes the wrong things and discards the right things.

The two main drivers—vision (growth) and operations (cost/efficiency)—can be identified by the questions they address. Vision-driven transformation asks:

- What are our future market realities?
- What is our preferred future state?
- What capabilities will we need to achieve that state?
- How do we design a comprehensive program for achieving our vision?
- What are the gaps between the desired and the actual and how do we close them?

At a U.S.-based fast-food restaurant chain, management's vision centered on improving the profitability of existing operations and on designing the restaurant of the future in line with growing the business. At a successful U.S. direct marketer of clothing and accessories, management wanted to improve customer retention, grow its base of customers, and establish new segments in the clothing industry.

Operations-driven transformation asks:

- How can we achieve operational excellence?
- How can we exploit our current capabilities?
- What new market opportunities can we pursue/create with these capabilities?
- Which opportunities do we want to pursue?
- What is the impact of these decisions on our future business and organization?

At a major U.S. bank, the operations driver was check processing. Operationally, the bank needed to design check processes that generated and sustained competitive advantage. A Northeast utility approached transformation on a company-wide basis in order to respond to deregulation and to become more competitive in serving customer preferences.

Whether the driver is vision or operations, the litmus test of effective process-centric management is flexibility. It is the opposite of company domination by functions, which often stand in the way of getting the job done by remaining rigid and unchanging in a changing environment, thereby making the firm pay the price for not keeping up. Processes succeed because they change company activities to match changes in the environment. They enable a company to keep up with what's happening in the marketplace. Flexibility is measured in terms of how quickly and how extensively a firm responds to change by restructuring and retooling.

When flexibility is not an integral part of process design and redesign, targets (e.g., financial objectives) are at high risk. Firms establish processes in order to keep up with continuous change; an unchanging process contradicts the process' reason to exist. Flexibility means that a process is neither ingrained nor hardwired. It involves connecting and reassembling building blocks to create value. Both management and the people directly involved in a process must continually monitor changes in their business situation and always be ready to change accordingly. In the ongoing dynamic, it is necessary to foresee the need and/or opportunity to change, to initiate a response, to manage the response, and to embed it in the fabric of the firm.

Rather than adopting a wait-and-see mindset, transforming firms develop scenarios and put them in play as part of strategic thinking. Management must anticipate new market-caused requirements and react to events that affect the business. Flexibility is at one extreme, certainty and predictability at the other. The more certain the needs and the list of events influencing the business is collected and understood, the more appropriate it is to stay on course. In contrast, the less certain the outlook, the more flexibility the firm must have, along with anticipatory and performance measurements that will provide important signals to make adjustments or, when necessary, implement radical changes.

All along the line, the reward system must create and support a corporate culture of skilled, motivated, and responsive people. They are the ones who work together in teams and become translators of information from various sources into knowledge of what's happening and what is likely to happen. They enable the firm to anticipate and recognize relevant change and to respond quickly to customer needs. It is in *their* direction that the reward system must flow—in the forms of compensation, awards, promotions, and recognition.

The hallmark of a process-centered organization is continuous improvement by drawing on workable approaches. Unfortunately, the technique that has been in the forefront of change—reengineering—has suffered from misunderstanding, unrealistic expectations, and simplistic application. Critics can lose sight of the formal definition drawn up by Michael Hammer and James Champy: "Reengineering is the fundamental rethinking and radical redesign of business processes to achieve dramatic improvements in critical, contemporary measures of performance, such as cost, quality, service, and speed." In identifying the "four key words" in this definition—*fundamental, radical, dramatic,* and *processes*—these authors single out the "most important" word in the definition: processes.[1]

We regard reengineering as a process technique that enables firms to achieve dramatic improvements by transforming the way they operate and do business. But this transformation doesn't occur in a vacuum. Reengineering depends on a number of crucial factors:

- a compelling reason to change,
- a commitment to making radical changes and to overcoming resistance aimed at reducing the scope of processes,
- a pervasive customer point of view,
- concrete goals to measure progress toward the end target, and
- committed leadership that drives change from the top down.

Hammer has cited the "spectacular benefits [of process work] for companies in a wide variety of industries."[2] Among the real-world examples he describes:

- John Deere Waterloo began managing order fulfillment as a process, increasing on-time deliveries to 99 percent, cutting inventory as a percentage of sales by two-thirds, and increasing market share by 90 percent.

- GTE identified and redesigned its service restoral process so that over 70 percent of all customer calls are resolved with only "one touch" by a company representative.

- Motorola managed and measured product development as an integrated process to reduce the time needed to bring new products to market by 80 percent.

- EDS created a strategic value selling process to muster and manage resources across its 45 business units so that it could pursue large business opportunities. In one year—1997—EDS closed more of these megadeals than it had in its entire 30-plus-year history.

Managing for Growth

When properly implemented and maintained, process management makes all the difference in managing a firm for growth. The stages of assessment and design prepare the way for a blueprint that contains several elements.

Vision and Goals. The firm must have a vision that is thought-out and developed in terms of the company's past, present, and, particularly, its future. The vision represents the value system of the firm, the commitment of top management, and the firm's position in the global marketplace. The vision cannot just hang on the wall. Management must link the vision to specific goals and timetables that are placed within a measurements framework. Measurements will ensure alignment of operations, activities, and decisions with corporate goals.

Typically, these measures are divided into categories in a "Balanced Business Scorecard":[3]

- *Financial*—how do we look to our shareholders?
- *Internal Perspective*—what business processes are the value drivers?
- *Organizational Learning*—are we able to sustain innovation, change, and improvement?
- *Customer Perspective*—how do we look to our customers?

When the measurements in a Balanced Business Scorecard show that vision and goals are aligned with business results, then processes can transform the way a firm does business. By providing a holistic snapshot of an organization's performance from both functional and process perspectives, this approach to measurements represents the most successful innovation in using business metrics in the past two decades

At Xerox, when Chairman and CEO Paul Allaire described the firm's shift to processes, his description resonated for all firms:

> You can't redesign processes unless you know what you're trying to do. What you're after is congruence among strategic direction, organizational design, staff capabilities, and the processes you use to ensure that people are working together to meet the company's goals. So you start by looking at the competition and reviewing your strategic direction, then you figure out how to organize to achieve the new goals."[4]

Common Processes. A firm must have a set of underlying, common processes that provide the stability of a single ecosystem. Such firm-wide "circuitry" promotes cooperation and coordination that go beyond geography, functions, departments, and divisions. While it doesn't happen overnight, once a firm is committed to common processes and the firm's top management supports this commitment, processes spread and are adopted throughout the firm. The processes must include common data elements, common measures of performance, and common linkages of information systems where people must work together across departments, disciplines, units, and geographical regions. For example, output in a discipline like marketing may be needed in another discipline like finance. The data must be accessible and understood across structural boundaries, as it must be across national boundaries.

As a new approach for translating high-level business strategy into operational strategy, market-based development (MBD) provides a framework for marshaling workflow processes to make the transition from a product-centric to a customer-/market-centric model. An integrated process for market management and product development is combined with a set of enablers—key principles representing industry best-of-breed practices and key measurements. The market management process provides the structure for managing a portfolio of offerings that address specific market segments. The product development process provides the structure for managing development of individual offerings.

In undergoing its own MBD transformation, IBM developed a new global business process and technology management structure that is aligned with corporate strategy. As an example, application planning and integration are now aligned with the business processes and groups they support. IBM Global Services has become the primary service provider and systems integrator for the company worldwide. Since implementing MBD, IBM has derived the following benefits with respect to computer hardware alone:

- Computer hardware development time has dropped from 48 months to 16 months.
- The number of hardware models has been reduced by more than 80 percent.
- The company has realized $155 million in benefits from using common building blocks.

Firm-Wide Process Management. Processes that are common to a firm require a firm-wide process leader who manages them and maintains links to other processes that are not universal. This involves standardizing data definitions and characteristics so that people are "talking the same language" and making decisions that are in alignment with each other. Included is the responsibility to develop uniform measurements of performance for each process implementer so that the firm can meaningfully interpret results, identify defects, and make improvements. This makes the process leader a key member of the business team; for this person, process management is a major (though not the total) area of responsibility.

At one major chemical company, a vice president allots half of his time to managing the customer order and inquiry fulfillment process. He devotes one-fourth of his time to strategic studies and leadership development and one-fourth to managerial responsibilities as a member of the office of the president, as chairman of a subsidiary, and as the executive responsible for new business development.

Process leaders must overcome organizational obstacles that develop over time, typically as fiefdoms and sacred cows. Such obstacles become parts of a firm that do not serve the whole, and they can even get in the way of overall strategy and goals. Inside the firm, units, brands, channels, and divisions can proliferate and go their particular ways. Whether or not they do a good job according to company metrics is beside the point if customers looking from the outside see lack of coordination, overlapping, or even chaos. Top management must identify this problem and support process leaders in eliminating it—both in appearance and in reality.

Team Play. A firm's reward system can make or break the team play that process requires. From compensation to recognition, the more team players are rewarded, the more they will participate and the louder is the message on what counts in the firm. When the compensation system has a bias for performance on project teams, people will strive to develop the skills that give them the best chance to be selected for teams and to operate effectively in those teams.

Applications. The primary purpose of and the greatest leverage provided by simplified business processes is the ability to incorporate modern information technology solutions into the workplace. To neglect such a powerful opportunity to develop and implement processes not only ignores sound management practices, but also endangers a firm's competitive position. At IBM, extensive analysis led to the process-managed strategy of Customer Relationship Management (CRM) to govern all activities related to customers. This strategy is not limited to Sales and Distribution, though that is where CRM was initially developed. It applies to everyone within IBM and to its business partners whose work touches customers. For IBM, CRM became established as "how we operate."

CRM emerged from a 1993 analysis that identified seven key areas for improving sales and delivery performance as the basis for establishing operational goals and implementing processes. Characterized as customer imperatives, these key areas are crucial to CRM and are readily recognized for their importance:

- cost/price,
- ease of doing business with IBM,
- fulfilling commitments,
- understanding the customer,

- competence,
- responsiveness/accessibility, and
- communication.

When translated into goals, these key areas lead to a clear set of dictates, meaning that customers have global access to a single IBM company that deploys the right skills at the right time and at the right cost. Add to this mix global channels focused on marketing strategies and transaction cycles that fit market conditions and customer wants and needs. The ultimate goal is to provide customers with the full benefits of boundaryless, worldwide sharing of IBM resources and information. To make this happen, a number of processes come into play. Those processes center on management of markets, skills, customer relations, opportunities, information, supply, business partners, and messages to the marketplace. Other processes encompass solution design and delivery and customer satisfaction.

Clearly, the effort and the commitment of resources were formidable, just as the results were impressive. At the end of 1997, IBM reported the results of CRM:

- For 110,000 opportunities worldwide, opportunity owners were assigned within 72 hours.
- Of 52,600 customer complaints logged, 93 percent had action plans in place within seven days.
- A total of $117 billion in potential business was identified to assist in achieving a year-end revenue plan of $76 billion.

Leadership. No vision and no set of goals will get anywhere without leadership at the top. That's where the results-oriented responsibility rests to provide focus for any organization's vision statement. Goal setting directs company efforts toward that vision in tangible, measurable terms. Top management leads the company toward goals based on extensive knowledge of the markets, the competition, and the firm's core competencies, values, and principles. In fulfilling its role, top management must be open to "scenario playing" to determine directions to go, markets to pursue, opportunities to seize.

To assess the firm's implementation of processes, management must ask several highly targeted questions. The answers will reveal what the firm has accomplished and what it still needs to do:

- Has the company appointed a process leader (a single accountable manager)?
- Has the company documented the process mission and scope?
- Is the current process documented? Do people follow it?
- Has the company explicitly defined and documented cross-organizational responsibilities for the process and the process elements, and do people throughout the company understand those responsibilities?
- Has the company allocated adequate resources? Are the proper skill levels in place? Is training/education adequate?
- Does the process leader have sufficient decision-making authority or escalation capability to ensure that process objectives are met?
- Has the process leader established a committee or advisory council to regularly review the status of the process and the latest measurements, analyze problems, and take action to improve results?
- Is the firm budgeting by process?

The Outcome

The firm that becomes process-centered keeps its balance. Processes are in sync with other aspects of doing business—specifically:

- capabilities such as functions/disciplines/skill sets,
- geographical differences,
- specific needs of customers and markets,
- inherent distinctions among products, and
- the P&Ls of the firm's various businesses.

The significant change is recognition of processes as a major part of the organization and establishment of an ongoing program to set up and maintain processes. Instead of processes emerging haphazardly, they become the result of conscious planning and allocation of resources. They receive the priority attention of top management and are an integral part of the firm and the way it does business. Previously, a process might emerge somewhere down the organizational pyramid as the result of individual initiative; now, a process becomes a conscious option when management is faced with problems or is seeking new initiatives.

Process-centric management takes a holistic approach toward change. And by responding proactively and rapidly, it keeps pace with the marketplace and positions itself to stay ahead of the competition. Demands and decisions are integrated as part of an ongoing transformation. Specifically, this ties together:

- *External Demands*—customer and competitor trends; environmental and socio-economic shifts; legislative trends; and other change drivers that materialize, depending on prevailing conditions.
- *Executive Decisions*—business direction and strategy, strategic imperatives, and strategic choices.
- *Decisions About Transformation*—shared/grounded vision, major transformation projects, major change enablers, and business operations structure.
- *Performance Measurement*—linking performance improvements to transformation projects and assessing the success of such projects.

As depicted in Figure 8-2, a real-time or dynamic approach continuously analyzes external drivers and conditions that may shape or change management decisions on strategy, investments, and marketplace choices. As top management monitors and takes in information through various channels, makes decisions on how the information impacts *what* the firm does, *when*, *where*, and *how*. When an organization has made the effort and has succeeded in implementing process, the three c's of process become evident in process leaders (cooperation), teams (coordination), and technology (communication).

Process leaders have end-to-end responsibility for creating and improving integrated design, providing supporting capabilities, instructing and supporting performers, and advocating for the process. Teams enable people to work together to find solutions, conduct activities, and produce measurable results. Technology provides information and tools for process management and the communications wherewithal so that cross-functional systems support processes in an integrated fashion.

The outcome is a process-centric firm that passes the "everyone test":

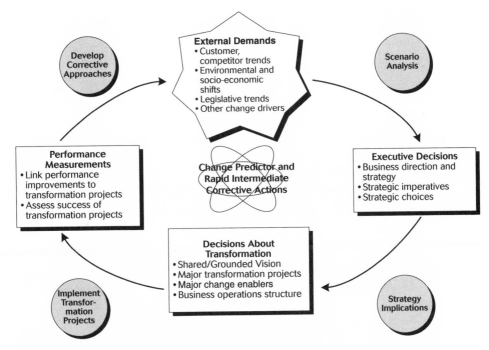

FIGURE 8-2. A HOLISTIC APPROACH

- Everyone knows the organization's processes—names, purposes, and interrelationships.
- Everyone knows where he or she fits in—the purpose and context for the particular job, the tasks performed, and the connection with the organization's goals.
- Everyone knows who's responsible for the processes—and the answer never is "nobody."
- Everyone knows what customers want and need—people share a coherent focus.
- Everyone is measured in terms of processes—under process-centric management systems.
- Everyone's head is turned 90 degrees—looking out, not up.

Summary

When firms become proficient at implementing processes and delivering value to their customers, they move beyond individual process management systems, which are often disconnected from important parts of the organization. They instead make the next leap forward to link process-based improvements to process-based transformation of the entire firm. They integrate transformation and strategy so that all decision makers view the same information as the basis for planning and action that create competitive advantages. This is not once-and-for-all change, but continuous activity that makes adjustments and mid-course corrections by relying on information technology as a crucial enabler and the glue that holds operations together. Information technology provides the speed and totality of execution that are crucial to transformation in a fast-changing market.

Yet technology, which is crucial and always on the minds of managers, often is not exploited to its full potential. In the context of transformation, technology is appropriately viewed in strategic—not technical—terms. Such is the approach of the next two chapters.

For Further Reading

Liam Fahey and Robert M. Randall, *Learning from the Future* (New York: John Wiley & Sons, 1998).

A valuable reference book on how companies are using scenarios.

Jay R. Galbraith, *Designing Organizations* (San Francisco: Jossey-Bass Publishers, 1995).

An executive briefing on strategy, structure, and process.

Michael Hammer and Steve Stanton, *The Reengineering Revolution: A Handbook* (New York: HarperBusiness, 1995).

A practical guide to process reengineering.

Michael Hammer, *Beyond Reengineering* (New York: HarperBusiness, 1996).

An update on reengineering and a look ahead at what happens after reengineering.

Robert S. Kaplan and David P. Norton, *The Balanced Scorecard* (Boston: Harvard Business School Press, 1996).

This book is the culmination of nearly a decade's worth of research and writing on the topic. IBM's own use of these techniques in hundreds of consulting engagements has demonstrated the value of Balanced Scorecards.

Frank Ostroff, *The Horizontal Organization* (New York: Oxford University Press, 1999).

A thorough report on managing organizations through process.

Part Four

LEVERAGING TECHNOLOGY

9

Working Partners:
Strategy and Technology

The Web offers companies the opportunity to
deliver either all or a substantial portion of
their business activities directly on line.
—Jeff Papows, CEO, Lotus

*This chapter presents a framework for applying technology
strategically by tying together value propositions and company
capabilities. It shows how IT strategy can change industries and
firms' practices and lead to new levels of profitability.*

In the early 1980s, when the AMR Corporation began its frequent flyer program to build customer loyalty, airline passengers were its customers, air travel its product. In the late 1990s, thirty million frequent flyers later, the AMR vision reflects the change in business strategy that information technology makes possible: "We will be the global leader in air transportation and related information services." A vision built on a strong partnership between business and information technology now encompasses American Airlines/American Eagle, AMR Global Services for the airline industry, AMR Investments for institutional and retail markets, and The Sabre Group.

The lead writer of this chapter is William A. Tulski, Jr.

159

As a widely recognized model of how IT can add value, The Sabre Group now defines its offerings as products and services across the full spectrum of travel. Its electronic distribution provides travel information, including schedules, availability, and fares, drawn from hundreds of travel suppliers. The information is available to travel agents, corporations, and online consumers twenty-four hours a day, 365 days a year. Sabre, which has one of the world's largest privately owned computer systems, also provides travel suppliers with IT solutions, specialized consulting, and technology outsourcing.

In December 1997, when American Airlines and Citibank announced a new platinum card as an addition to the Citibank AAdvantage brand of credit cards, the statement by Kevin Kessinger, general manager of the program, spoke about IT's ongoing role in creating value by serving customers:

> Citibank and American Airlines teamed up over ten years ago to introduce what quickly became the most popular frequent flier credit card program in the industry. Since that introduction, constant innovation and responsiveness to the marketplace have ensured our leadership position and card members who are among the most loyal in the industry. The introduction of the Citibank Platinum Select AAdvantage card, with its enhanced benefits and services, is just another demonstration of our commitment to servicing these card members' needs."[1]

The AMR Corporation is doing what other firms are doing and what many others can do. The starting premise is that firms have unprecedented opportunities to use information technology in their strategy to retain and gain customers by expanding and adding products and services. Management teams that capitalize on these opportunities identify their firms' capabilities, analyze what's happening in the external environment, and explore the technologies that exist to deliver results for their firm. It's not about achieving marginal rates of return, but about gaining a leadership role in an industry or business segment. Picking technologies off the shelf often is an insufficient (however popular) strategy because it does not separate a company from the competition, particularly in the global marketplace, where copycat products pop up all over the world. As in chess, firms compete so that over time they will dominate—and not just share a part of—the board.

What counts is assembling technological capabilities that are infused with company strategy and vision and that capitalize on the company's strong points. The goals are a distinctive place in the marketplace and competitive advantage, as AMR has done in thinking through what it could do with customer information and loyalty. AMR did this by targeting market segments, pricing differently to appeal to different customers, and spawning additional services by identifying other uses for information the firm already has. The more AMR capitalizes on its information advantage, the greater the barrier to present and potential competitors.

Transforming Entire Industries

Sabre is more than a single firm's success story. It is an impressive and well-referenced example of the impact of information flow on an entire industry. Sabre brought the travel industry into the Information Age through the foresight and effort of American Airlines. It also exemplifies the way an IT-based innovation in one industry can trigger similar innovations in other industries.

Frequent flyer programs, now a part of virtually every airline's value propositions, became one of many natural evolutionary steps that have occurred in the past twenty years in which information about the customer is used to get closer to the customer. Co-branded credit cards with expanded services have appeared in other industries as well. In the United States, both Ford and GM have developed credit card programs to build up credits toward vehicle purchases. Banks in Latin America and Western Europe are implementing similar strategies. Such programs help expand the relationship with the customer and simultaneously provide an enriched information source to guide a continuing stream of new offerings.

What happened in the travel industry occurred earlier than in other industries because it is so information-dependent. Schedules and prices are the most significant drivers in customer purchases, and the industry depends on a complex network of reservation and inventory systems involving transportation and accommodations. A number of interconnected but competing reservation and inventory systems have been developed and supported by the major carriers, such as Galileo, Worldspan, Amadeus, and Apollo. For hotels, systems such as Pegasus and THISCO provide reservation services and availability information. Overall, there are upwards of 700 airlines, fifty rental car companies, and more than 34,000 hotels in over 95 hotel chains that plug into these systems.[2] The systems are accessed by about 32,000 travel agents in the U.S. and about 66,000 travel agents worldwide. These are mostly small businesses that must compete with direct sales by the carriers and chains, by at least four major online travel services, and by smaller online services.

Predictably, Microsoft identified the information factor in the travel industry and elsewhere in its strategic planning: "We are challenging old and established businesses like newspapers, travel agencies, automobile dealers, entertainment guides, travel guides, Yellow Page directories, magazines, and, over time, many other areas. We must devise ways of working with them or winning away their customers and revenue streams."[3]

Microsoft, which announced its intention to enter the travel business in 1994, launched Expedia.com in December 1996 in partnership with Worldspan, a firm that offers computerized reservation services and that in turn is partly owned by Northwest and Delta. Expedia.com includes hotel, rental, and air travel reservations and ticketing in what shapes up as a challenge to travel agencies. By the end of 1997, Expedia.com had booked $100 million in travel revenues and was already one of the largest online travel businesses.

Preview Travel, Travelocity, and Internet Travel Network are three others, each with an IT-based strategy. Preview Travel presents itself as a source of consumer-driven, unbiased, comparative shopping via a Web page with four million registered subscribers. Along with Travelocity, it aims at the online business and leisure customer segments by offering services built on information-based capabilities. Internet Travel Network, which started in 1995, aims at providing an online presence to travel agents with a site designed to provide travelers with Web searching while continuing a relationship with their travel agents for booking and inquiries.

While the major firms in online travel services may pursue different strategies, they employ similar capabilities in a convergence of technologies, industry infrastructure, and information, and they follow similar patterns in merging with other parts of the industry. They are providing all the scheduling, pricing, and availability information a purchaser needs to make comparisons and buy a ticket. They can make reservations, accept payments, and send tickets, as well as provide convenient facilities to revise travel itineraries with 24-by-7 access.

The impact of these online services is already evident in commission and fee structures. Online services pay a charge for each inquiry they make for scheduling and availability and for making reservations. The information, which is managed and updated by its users, derives its value from accuracy and timeliness. Meanwhile, commission rates have already dropped to 5 percent for online providers, reflecting a judgment on the part of the carriers that the online services are more efficient and have a lower cost structure than traditional channels. The drop in their commissions can be viewed as a claim on the surplus created by the more efficient channel.

Travel agents, whose traditional commission was 10 percent, now earn roughly 8 percent, with a $50 cap per ticket. Some carriers allow as little as 5 percent with a $25 cap and still others have a flat fee of $15 per ticket. In response, travel agents—who declined in number by 6 percent in 1997—took steps to improve their position by responding in kind. USTAR, the U.S. Travel Agency Registry, has an online site with an information system called Genesis. The goal is to serve the collective needs of travel agents and reduce their dependence on carriers and other information providers in the industry.[4]

The information-based shift in who adds value has wide-ranging consequences that already stand out in sales and marketing. The more customers gain direct access to information and the more buying they can do directly, the less they need intermediaries. They enter a world of "do-it-yourself" information gathering and consumer purchasing, thereby eroding the role of agents who find information and sell to customers. The challenge to sales and marketing strategies across the marketplace is already well-advanced in real estate, financial trading, and insurance. The questions to be faced are at the heart of doing business: *Do we really need salespersons? What is their role in the information revolution? How do we convert what is happening with information into a competitive advantage? What can we learn from what is happening in our industry and in other industries?*

While not all technological changes are as pervasive and far-reaching as those in the travel industry, all firms, including those in smokestack industries, feel the impact and can find opportunities stemming from the strategic use of information technology. Chaparral Steel in Midlothian, Texas, is a striking example. The company uses information technology to mix and match its products in response to changing market conditions and customer requirements. The company, which produces bar and structural steel products by recycling scrap steel, can customize each bar of steel it produces. Customer-focused production delivers exactly the steel customers want, with the exact combination of chemicals, manganese, cobalt, and other ingredients. The result is a highly competitive product that is customized at low cost, with minimum waste and maximum quality. The company does more than keep up with its customers. By capitalizing on information capabilities, it can anticipate their needs.

In the paper industry, Madison Paper Industries in Madison, Maine uses IT to balance the critical drivers of efficiency in the mill—long runs and few changeovers—with customer needs for different weights and dimensions of paper, which pull in the opposite direction. Like its competitors, the company faced tough tradeoffs in minimizing waste in the paper trimming operation and in assembling orders for delivery. Wasted space in the trucks and wasted paper trimmings mean higher costs and higher prices for the customer. At the same time, the company does not want to compromise speed in delivering products or force customers to take a product that does not suit their needs. The company wants to carry out its intentions for service delivery in real time at the point of taking a customer's order. By using information technology to optimize load planning and to analyze the options for servicing demand, the company enables its people to deliver better results faster—with savings in the millions of dollars.[5]

Management Rethinking

Because business opportunities that were once not possible or cost-effective have become both practical and profitable thanks to information technology, management faces the challenge of rethinking, redefining, and repositioning its business. This calls for an understanding of the marketplace possibilities, an assessment of the risks of failure with any proposed initiative, and a sound projection of returns. Each of these tasks is a complicated challenge that does not abide simple solutions. As a result, most firms are in a strenuous learning phase at the same time as many achieve significant successes with IT initiatives. Given the acknowledged pace of change, firms need to reevaluate much of the conventional wisdom and traditional strategy and reapply it to the new world of information-driven business.

IBM's experience with a wide range of firms in different industries confirms that companies are moving ahead successfully with information technology rather than hesitating in the face of any debate over a "productivity paradox." The debate developed when economists tried to link investments in IT to observable gains in productivity at the macro-economic level. Researchers reported—paradoxically—that IT investments correlated with a decline in productivity. This is counter-intuitive in view of all the advantages technology brings to a business and the documented successes brought about by deploying IT over the past half-century.

The debate goes on, even about whether the traditional computations used to produce the paradox are relevant. In recent research by MIT Professor Erik Brynjolfsson and others, new variables emerged in studies of firms that realized positive business returns on IT. When the research focused on what must be done to make IT investments pay off, positive business returns correlated with such variables as the firm's IT skills investments, policies, incentive schemes, and similar factors.[6]

As a brief historical flashback to put the paradox in perspective, the introduction of the steam engine and electric power is instructive. Engineers first used these advances simply to replace hydro-power systems. But the biggest boosts in productivity came when power plants were deployed to allow the actual work flows to be redesigned. This is a story of human learning about how to improve and optimize physical operations, first in the details, then at the system level, and, most recently, across enterprises.

Information technology is a different matter. It has a different focus.

It helps organizations manipulate and communicate data, information, and maybe even knowledge. At this point, there is a gap in know-how: understanding of how to manipulate materials and objects in the physical world is far greater than understanding of thinking and communication processes.[7]

How much does the "productivity paradox" debate affect IT decisions in a particular firm? In our judgment, not much at all. Individual firms aren't focused on changing the value of an hour of labor. They're focused on the value provided to their customers. In this light, the discussion of macro-economic productivity has limited relevance. It has been clear for some time that firms must couple IT investments with appropriate skills and management systems, relate them to a business vision and focus, integrate them into the existing business, and link them to the customer. IBM consultants have found that investments in IT and any related uncertainties are not comprehensively analyzed in terms of macro-economic productivity.

Management must gamble to a certain degree with IT, but that does not mean betting the business. IT investments in most companies amount to only about 2 percent to 4 percent of sales, whereas profit margins in sales after taxes run 10 percent or 11 percent. So in the worst-case scenario, a setback in a technology gamble would have only a limited, near-term impact, to be weighed against the payoff of getting far ahead of the competition in the long haul. The issue is no longer about whether to invest in IT, but how to transform the business to pursue a new information-based vision—one that gets ahead of the competition. This is the essential partnership between IT and strategy.

In a study sponsored by the National Science Foundation and IBM, scholars at the University of California at Berkeley are examining IT productivity from three perspectives: process, the company, and the national economy. Evidence to date strongly confirms that the more than $5 billion spent globally on IT has yielded important value across all three dimensions. It also confirms the validity of Thomas Davenport's advice of several years ago that companies must reengineer processes to exploit IT capabilities.[8]

For firms that are transforming themselves, strategy has become a multi-sided fusion of vision, technology, resources, and processes that can produce explosive business returns when focused on delivering value to customers. Information technologies can help establish barriers to competitors, bestow first-mover advantages, establish a head start in capturing the market, provide additional distinction to a brand, and accelerate the development and application of know-how. None of these results occurs for free, however; they all take extensive work and a focused approach—not much new there.

What is relatively new and is still emerging is an overall understanding of three major elements: the firm as a collection of distinctive capabilities, the market as ever more finely segmented by detailed wants and needs, and the future as spanning an analyzable range of critical possibilities.[9] That's why earlier chapters in this book focused on knowledge management, competencies, and Customer Value Management as future-oriented building blocks of enterprises. In working with customers and within the company, IBM consultants find that the payoff is greatest when clients consider all three as an integrated set rather than as discrete parts that the company must coordinate.[10]

Most firms seeking an edge do not limit themselves to one initiative; they experiment and explore on several fronts, creating a portfolio of technological ventures. In doing so, management teams address a number of key questions for each initiative:

- What value will the firm deliver? To whom?
- Which business capabilities will form the basis of delivering this value? Will these capabilities establish a competitive advantage in the future?
- What resources will the company need? How will the company develop these resources and make them operational and efficient?
- What roles will IT play? At what cost? With what potential returns?
- What are the risks involved? What risks is the firm able and ready to undertake?
- Can the firm develop technologies that will be unique for a significant period of time?
- Does it make sense to acquire critical capabilities or to create partnerships to share the benefits of technology?

These questions encompass the necessary and sufficient elements of the strategy for a venture: value propositions, capabilities, and resources. In all firms, as strategy aims at producing something of value to the customer, management has the task of identifying the capabilities and resources needed to make that value a reality in the marketplace. For most firms, strategy must also consider the suitability of what's already on hand, as in the examples previously cited: Madison Paper's pursuit of breakthrough levels of customer service, Chaparral Steel's micro customization, and AMR's travel-related, information-based products. Like so many other enterprises, these firms used IT to complement and expand their existing capabilities to deliver value to customers. They invested in the resources (hardware, systems, and staffing) needed to support new initiatives in a technology/strategy plan.[11]

Starting with the capabilities and resources of the firm, management needs a framework for making choices and acting on marketplace-based decisions. The questions behind the decisions go to the core of competition:

- Why provide these offerings for these customers as opposed to exploring other potentially productive uses of the firm's capabilities by other customers?
- What does the future hold in the marketplace?
- How can and should the company plan its investments in technology to position itself to compete successfully?

The ultimate answers to these questions come from the customer—but a significantly different customer, one who more than ever is informed and empowered. The answer that counts is whether the customer does or does not buy.

Value Propositions and Attributes

Value propositions, the starting point for a decision-making framework, take the form of a general statement of customer benefits that a business delivers. As the integration of many features of business became the norm in the 1990s (e.g., process design, use of IT), value propositions helped managers "keep their eye on the ball." In general, marketing- or advertising-oriented messages such as "everyday low price" or "large selection" were and still are good starting points for creating value propositions. For customers, these statements help to identify what a firm is offering. For AMR, the statement could be: *We not only provide air travel, but also all the information and arrangements travelers need to get the most out of their trip in terms of cost and convenience.* For Chaparral Steel: *We produce and deliver steel that is customized to customer needs.* For Madison Paper: *We produce the paper customers want when they want it.*

Value attributes go further. They set forth the specifics of an offering, the basis for buyers' evaluations of how their needs and wants are met. Typically, the attributes have positive value—a reason to buy. At times, however, management may decide not to match the competition in certain attributes. These are "negatively valued attributes," which managers identify as not crucial. They are not the "attractors/differentiators," which win new customers for the company as part of Customer Value Management (described in Chapter 3).

Choices on what attributes not to provide can be as important as choices on what attributes to provide. The accepted norms of competition may prompt suppliers to deliver attributes that are no longer valuable to their customers or that are not valuable to a specific market. When attributes survive beyond their relevance for all or part of their market, opportunities emerge for a competitor with a fresh approach who sheds such attributes, saves money, and carves out a niche in the market. Southwest Airlines is a compelling example of productive choices about what not to deliver along with what to deliver in a focused offering. As far back as 1985, the company ran an ad entitled "The Company Plane": "... A schedule that dovetails beautifully with your own. With first-rate service that includes complimentary beverages. And everyday fares that are so low it's almost like flying for free. Because our flights are so convenient, our service so attentive, and our fares so low, business people actually think of us as the company plane...."[12]

While all airlines claim to offer convenience, service, and low prices, Southwest came up with its own version of these general statements of value with an eye on business travelers. For Southwest, service focused on attention and beverages, but not meals (which many seasoned travelers do not value highly). What kind of customer will give Southwest a try? A traveler who has experienced one too many airplane meals but might like a cup of coffee on the flight and who values the availability of frequent flights and cost savings. Southwest set its sights—successfully—on the loyalty of repeat business by accentuating what it identified as positive attributes and by setting aside negative ones.

Figure 9-1 depicts Southwest's *value propositions* (low price and convenience), its *positive value attributes* (pricing; direct purchasing; frequent departures; first-come, first-served seating; best baggage handling record; and uncongested airports if possible), and its *negative value attributes* (no refunds for lost tickets, frequent flyer restrictions, no premium services, no meals). Analysis of such value attributes provides the key to identifying and serving particular markets and dominating specific niches.

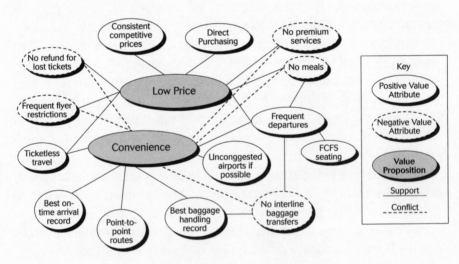

FIGURE 9-1. SOUTHWEST AIRLINES' VALUE PROPOSITIONS

In another example, a comparison of online book selling by Amazon.com and Barnes & Noble shows how two firms with the same value propositions can differ on specific value attributes:

• *Online book searching and buying*—Both firms are similar in the searching process but differ on access to book reviews.

- *Online book reviewer community*—Amazon is open to all, while Barnes & Noble requires a registration, albeit a very simple one.
- *Repeat purchasing incentives*—Both companies offer account setup. Amazon is adding other classes of products, while Barnes & Noble has added technology-based user conveniences.
- *Purchase delivery*—Both companies use such services as UPS, USPS, FedEx, etc., with similar shipping charges and delivery times.
- *Chat, book signings, and other author events*—Virtually identical for both companies.

Amazon.com, Barnes & Noble, and Southwest Airlines illustrate the process of identifying what a firm wants to offer customers with a view to how customers will evaluate, acquire, and use proposed offerings. What counts with customers is a company that looks outward as prelude to looking inward at what it can deliver.

Identifying Capabilities

Armed with a strategic view of intended offerings to customers, firms can move ahead to identify their capabilities—what the firm can do— as the basis for delivering on their intentions. Capabilities, which include people and their knowledge, also rely on well-deployed information technologies along with processes and policies directed at accomplishing some or all of the firm's value propositions. As set forth in Chapters 4, 5, and 6, knowledge is applied to a specific end (support of value propositions or other capabilities) through a set of methods and processes. The knowledge component of a capability is increasingly becoming the obvious and decisive element. Clearly, if the relevant knowledge is commonplace or if a firm's methods are inefficient, its capabilities have little potential for providing competitive advantage. On the other hand, if the knowledge is more or less limited to the company or if the company's methods are more efficient, a capability can offer competitive advantage, which will show up in marketplace results.

A firm typically develops capabilities over time in adaptation to its changing value propositions. The firm normally derives its economic advantage from rarity or scarcity. Capabilities that are distinctive to a company are often difficult for competitors to appropriate or imitate, accounting for competitive advantage—the classic Michael Porter position.[13] Recent research also suggests that industries that are highly dependent on technology or scientific knowledge (e.g., pharmaceuticals, computer industries) also have the same kinds of experiences with knowledge, capabilities, and strategic applications of information technology.[14]

In its consulting work, IBM frequently works with clients who want to look at the interrelationships among sets of a firm's capabilities in order to study the ways in which they support or conflict with each other. This can lead to the identification of patterns of alignment, segregation, integration, and reinforcement that can produce competitive advantages. Usually, most of a firm's capabilities are directed toward delivering the value propositions currently accepted by customers. Sometimes they are directed at inventing, developing, or evaluating some new set of value propositions, such as those made possible by e-business. In other cases, companies focus on delivering value propositions to new constituencies, as Southwest did with business travelers. Because Southwest decided to deliver convenience according to its own specific definition, it could cut costs stemming from meals, managing interline baggage, and premium services—capabilities not highly valued by the customers targeted. Eliminating these capabilities helped in other ways as well. Southwest could turn planes around faster at the gate, allowing more dense schedules and better utilization of the company's aircraft.

However, a close look at Southwest's low prices and convenience points to a potential conflict. At some point, additional services for customer convenience would require higher operating costs and prices. This also would involve choices about what to eliminate—choices best made on the basis of the wants and needs of specific market segments. A firm must first decide on the customers it will serve, then study what they want (as described in earlier chapters) and analyze its own capabilities in deciding what it will and will not deliver. Just as IT played a major role in enabling Southwest to identify and analyze the customers it was targeting and to adjust its resources to deliver particular value, IT also becomes a major player in choosing what attributes offer positive value and make a competitive difference.

For most firms in practically all industries, management must continually reformulate value propositions to remain competitive and to preserve the company's differentiation from its competition. The trick is to develop capabilities that support the evolution of value propositions and to deliver them economically. This creates a dynamic tension. As a firm continually refines its capabilities in order to deliver today's value propositions, it must retain the flexibility to changes in value propositions.

In the pressure to keep up with both customers and competition, information technologies can speed development of a firm's knowledge base through processing (sorting, ordering, filtering, and organizing) massive amounts of raw data the firm accumulates. This process lays important groundwork for knowledge generation and sharing, decision making, and productive innovation. As exemplified by Madison Paper, the company's systems sift through the myriad combinations of possible truck load and order delivery schedules to identify those that are most likely to satisfy the broadest set of customer needs. The systems codify operating rules and filter what had previously been done manually—with far greater speed and mastery of complicated data.

IT also aids in the efficient execution of processes that put knowledge into practice and help improve the way capabilities support each other. It's important to note that while IT is an enabler, people continue to play the crucial roles of providing the knowledge content of a capability and of deciding how to use resources in serving market needs.

Summary

Whatever the firm or industry, information technology continues to open up new and expansive ways of thinking about possibilities in the marketplace and of acting upon them. As new forms of computing and communication become available (e.g., the Internet), IT makes products and services possible in fundamentally different shapes and forms by combining speed and range with unprecedented access to information. Information storage and retrieval continue to become ever more economical and easy, while processing grows more powerful and sophisticated. It's no accident that we are seeing a profound shift to digitally based commerce as significant as the development of the Second Industrial Revolution driven by electricity and transportation.

We expect what we do today will be faster, cheaper, more pervasive, and more commonplace tomorrow. And that is the problem. It has become increasingly difficult to stop, look, and think about what has suddenly become feasible or economical to do and would be valued by someone if it were done. For management, the challenge is to maintain an early warning system that scans the horizon for technological developments, innovations, and major change in the making. The Internet is an obvious example, but there are many others. The expansiveness and detail of available information, the complexity of analysis that can be applied in ever shorter periods of time, the speed and pervasiveness of delivering results—these are the elements that make for revolutionary change.

Managers are learning the value of relating what is emerging technologically to the firm's strategy and response capabilities. This requires a clear, ongoing policy for mapping and dealing with the technologies of today while positioning the firm to capitalize on tomorrow's technologies—always within the broader framework already described. This calls for a balanced business perspective in viewing the latest and newest technology and in identifying what to look for in looking ahead—the focus of the next chapter.

For Further Reading

James W. Cortada, *Best Practices in Information Technology: How Corporations Get the Most Value from Exploiting Their Digital Investments* (Upper Saddle River, NJ: Prentice Hall PTR, 1998).

IBM consultant Cortada focuses the first four chapters on alignment of IT with business strategy, the theme of this chapter.

Steven L. Goldman, Roger N. Nagel, and Kenneth Preiss, *Agile Competitors and Virtual Organizations: Strategies for Enriching the Customer* (New York: Van Nostrand Reinhold, 1995).

A report on research done by the Iacocca Institute on how

American manufacturing firms were changing. A major study also useful to service firms.

Roy L. Harmon, *Reinventing the Business: Preparing Today's Enterprises for Tomorrow's Technology* (New York: Free Press, 1996).

One of the most important "post-reengineering" descriptions of how to think of IT strategically.

IBM Consulting Group, *Global Telecommunications to the Year 2000: The Impact on Corporate IT Strategies and Applications* (New York: Economist Intelligence Unit, 1996).

This survey of practices of corporations around the world flagged the rapid move toward e-business strategies. The cases are explicit and contemporary.

Jerry Luftman, *Competing in the Information Age: Strategic Alignment in Practice* (New York: Oxford University Press, 1996).

Written primarily by IBM consultants, this is a collection of papers on how to apply computing to business issues, strategies, and problems.

David B. Yoffie, *Competing in the Age of Digital Convergence* (Boston: Harvard Business School Press, 1997).

This is a large collection of case studies on exploiting digital technology, primarily in product development, services, and internal capabilities. An excellent anthology.

10

Technologies for Today and Tomorrow

*Only if you understand where technology is going will your
perspective on where your business can go be as broad
as possible and provide the greatest potential.*
—John Daniels and N. Caroline Daniels

*The key concepts in information technology provide the basis
for discussing its current and future deployment. Such a discussion benefits from the full range of experience in applying IT and
from extensive research on the framework and environment
that enable firms to get the most out of technology. Given the
rapid pace of IT development and the continuous stream of
innovation and breakthroughs, it is unrealistic to designate particular technologies as the dominant wave of the future. Instead,
four areas of research and development, which we review in
this chapter, stand out in looking ahead: computer interfaces,
collaboration/enablement, advanced processing, and connec-
tion/distribution.*

The shrinking of a "Web Year" in the late 1990s speaks volumes about the pace of change in technology. The developments in hardware, software, strategies, applications,
and management practices that cascade upon management

The lead writer of this chapter is William A. Tulski, Jr.

176

and its information technology operations have accelerated to the point where a "Web Year" is regarded as one month long. What happens in information technology in a 30-day period today matches what happened over the course of 12 months in the recent past. Keeping up has been compared to drinking from a fire hose that's shooting out water at full force.

For its part, management no longer needs convincing about the importance of information technology. The issues revolve around picking the right technologies and putting them to work at the right time—today and tomorrow. There is no way to generalize with assurance about the rate and types of change in IT, as PCs are replaced every year or two and their software applications are refreshed or replaced in cycles of less than one year. Most significantly, these changes are all interrelated, making it difficult to identify patterns of change.[1]

Meanwhile, the search to keep up never stops, as noted by an IBM Consulting Group report:

> Best practice companies that view information technology as a strategic enabler actively research and systematically evaluate new technologies. They typically have an advanced technology function to conduct targeted research, collaborate with business units on future needs, and ensure linkage to the enterprise architecture. They minimize new technology risks through a systematic approach to applied research for evaluating, prototyping, and piloting feasible technologies.[2]

In applying technology, firms must factor in change from inside and outside the organization. Firms are reengineering, restructuring, downsizing, acquiring, and globalizing. They are confronting the competition, coping with challenges in products and services, and monitoring upheaval in their industries. Executives and managers are operating in an environment of continuous adjustment, whether it be, for example, a utility firm dealing with privatization in its industry or a retail firm trailing the competition. Whatever the situation, IT is playing a major role in the adjustments firms are making. After the utility experienced a radical change from monopoly supplier to one among several rival providers, its CEO called upon IT to deliver a new set of systems in a hurry to underpin a new way of doing business and radical changes in the firm's culture, business processes, and cost structure. The CIO became the CEO's principal ally in driving fundamental changes by applying the right technology. At the retail firm, the CEO hired a CIO to come up with innovative use of IT in order to compete with entrenched rivals whom the firm could not match on the standard bases of competition. The CIO responded by propelling the firm forward in areas such as logistics and promotion management by developing lean systems that could be implemented in a few months and expanded over time.[3]

All firms face the same questions. Faced with a myriad of rapidly changing technologies, any of which might offer unprecedented competitive advantages, how can management identify the key differentiating technologies to use in an increasingly competitive marketplace? How can management keep pace with the technologies that are essential to maintaining competitive parity? How much change can organizations productively absorb?

Our view is that the search for answers does not begin by latching onto the latest technology, but by identifying and analyzing the capabilities that make significant differences in the marketplace. In going from point A to point B, management must determine what it needs: Does R&D need better understanding of customer interests? Does sales and marketing need better insights into customer buying patterns? Does upper management need to build new alliances with alternative channel partners or key research organizations?

As in a game of cards, with the unfolding of the game you can get a good idea of the cards your opponents hold while you know what you have and what you need for a winning hand. You can draw the winning cards, but so can the other side. In the marketplace, technology choices—rather than luck—can deliver winning cards. The outcome may or may not go to the players with the best hands. It depends on how well they play their cards. In business, technology is a powerful tool to do just that: it enables management to "play the game" with a strong, customer-oriented competitive strategy.

Sometimes, a single piece of information technology can be the crucial enabler. More often it is a portfolio of technologies. But whatever the case, management must make decisions in terms of the capabilities the company needs. The formula is straightforward: the ends (vision and strategy) dictate the means (technology).

Some Basics

As with "any form of computer-based information system, including mainframe as well as microcomputer applications," information technology represents a combination of computer hardware and software.[4] What, then, is an application? It is the deployment or implementation of IT within a firm to automate or facilitate the accomplishment of some task(s) that is (are) valuable to the firm. Our unit of analysis for IT is any system that is focused on an identifiable portion of a firm's work.

No IT application stands alone. As Powell and Dent-Micallef report in an extensive review of the factors contributing to successful implementation of IT, a firm needs an open organization, open communications, consensus, senior executive commitment, and flexibility.[5] Their research shows that in the absence of these supporting factors, IT alone cannot consistently deliver competitive advantages. In IBM's consulting experience, the knowledge component in applying IT includes knowledge of the firm as well as technology.

Within any company, IT applications benefit from complementarity and cospecialization.

Complementarity of resources describes the extra boost that occurs when two or more capabilities support each other. An example is the sustainable and significant advantage derived from an electronic data interchange (EDI) application when there is a strong level of trust between collaborating firms, whereas trust alone or an EDI system alone provides much less advantage. Cospecialization occurs when two (or more) capabilities must be present for a firm to derive some advantage and when little advantage occurs with only one or the other. An example is the capability to develop the Ivory Soap brand, which is very tightly linked to the development of the Ivory Soap product. Alone, either would be worth far less.

In the instance of an IT system for analyzing customer buying patterns, the system is critically dependent on the capability of acquiring data about customers. For the many firms that construct

Web sites to promote sales, it is necessary to integrate the Web sites into their order-entry systems—otherwise they won't be able to handle significant order volumes efficiently and profitably.

Other characteristics of resources and capabilities are also useful in understanding their value to firms. If a capability allows a firm to accomplish something valuable for its customers but is not deeply embedded among other complementary or cospecialized capabilities, then it is imitatable. It allows a competing firm to achieve competitive parity. A capability must be both rare and valuable to provide a firm with competitive advantage. The Ivory Soap brand, whose recognition for quality and purity is valued by customers, has been cultivated and developed for many years and is now a great advantage to its owner in branding related soap products. Capabilities can defy imitation when their advantage is hard to identify or if they require an accumulation of knowledge over a long period of time.

These basic characteristics affect all effective applications of IT, whether based on Internet e-business or a traditional centralized mainframe. As with knowledge and process-centric management, synergy plays a crucial role, as it has for decades.

Advances in IT

Because information technology is appropriately viewed as imbedded in a firm's set of interrelated business capabilities, no responsible management ignores advances in IT. There is no escape: the steady and rapid advancement of processing power, storage, memory, and display technology has made possible new applications that affect all firms. Microprocessors, memory devices, and many other kinds of specialized circuitry used in computers have benefited from the decreased size of faster and more powerful digital circuits. Although experts in solid state physics have predicted slowdowns in the face of fundamental limits, such problems have, thus far, been circumvented. IBM researchers estimate that the pace of progress will slow down "beginning perhaps ten years from now, or even sooner," with the projection that "the slope of progress will moderate, and the industry will have to advance in lower gear."[6] Industry progress in software development has been less dramatic than in hardware but is still advancing, especially with such recent developments as Java, which reportedly doubles development productivity in some cases.[7] We are on the verge, however, of very important advances in the development of software, which over the next decade should further increase the replacement of old applications.[8]

The impacts that generate the greatest interest create or enhance a firm's sustainable advantages and therefore deserve the most attention. Given the fragility of any forecast about a particular technology, we will focus on capability-oriented developments, specifically computer interfaces, collaboration/enablement, advanced processing, and connection/distribution applications. They are the building blocks of future IT uses. Each has a significant impact on business capabilities. Each affects competitive advantage. Each is represented by emerging technologies that point to future directions—technologies that will drive the kinds of change receiving press attention in reports on e-business, the Internet, and the "digital economy."

Computer Interfaces

Since the mid-1980s, the ways in which data move in and out of computers have changed dramatically. In the previous twenty years, computer input and output had been predominantly text-based, without much variation in the forms of text-based output: printed reports, line mode displays, and full-screen displays. Today, computer interfaces include graphical user interfaces (GUIs), high resolution, color, 2D and 3D graphics and image rendering, text-to-speech, voice and handwriting recognition, and scanning and optical character recognition.

Until recently, the computer keyboard itself had not changed much as the predominant input device for general and personal computing. It has now been augmented with the mouse and it now sends signals directly to the computer rather than through a cumbersome arrangement of card punch and reader.

But as specialized applications have demonstrated, we can devise much more efficient ways of getting much greater volumes of data into computers. These applications include MRIs in medical imaging, satellite and seismic sensors in geological exploration, and cash registers at retail points of sale. When we get larger volumes of data into the computer, we create the opportunity for powerful new applications with tremendous benefits. The key is finding vastly more sophisticated, efficient, and cost-effective means of data input.

Progress is on the way. As voice recognition continues to improve in accuracy and convenience, it provides a more effective means to input data and commands that now go through keyboards. This will significantly increase productivity, since people generally speak much faster than they type.[9] Research and development of new input interfaces goes further to encompass the richness of communications via gestures, gazes, facial expressions, and voice inflection.[10] These additional cues can dramatically modify spoken communication.[11] According to some measures, the words used in face-to-face dialogue constitute as little as 7 percent of the information we convey.[12] At IBM and at other labs, researchers are working on human-centered interfaces that attempt to recognize some of these additional cues and context,[13] enabling people to communicate with computers in ways that are natural and efficient. (Automated telephone directory systems have already become commonplace.) An explosion of data is in the offing, as these projects mature and enable computers to recognize and capture much more of what people communicate.

A third form of communication, handwriting, involves the powerful cultural, personal, and legal biases for handwritten forms. Signatures are required for checks and for most credit card transactions. In some settings, it is still deemed acceptable to write notes while unacceptable to clack away at a keyboard. Because paper forms are cheap and convenient, they are still used to gather information, which is then entered into a computer system for analysis. The resulting loss of productivity and other business impacts due to time delays and errors are well documented.[14] In response, there are a variety of products and applications available that allow a person's handwriting to be read dynamically[15] and that enable computers to automatically read forms.[16]

What is happening in computer output parallels what is happening in computer input. Technological developments have demonstrated in specialized, high-end applications what can be done, though presently at a much higher cost and therefore with limited deployment. The significant differentiators in output are the resolution of the image, the number of colors that can be displayed, and the rate of display. The majority of individual computer users work with a CRT or LCD screen, devices that are one to two square feet in surface area that usually provide color output at a resolution that still falls well short of photographs or other printed forms. At the high end, computer rendering is now routinely used to create special effects in the most visually demanding of applications, as in the Hollywood movie that is displayed on several hundred square feet of surface area to rave reviews.

Researchers are also developing ways for computers to speak, simulating the natural flow of words that marks a person's discourse. Computers will then synthesize natural-sounding speech as a necessary component of a speech-based interactive interface. Recent research has also shown that even non-interactive spoken instructions allow people to complete tasks in less than half the time of text-based written instructions.[17] The wide deployment of Voice Response Units (VRUs), typically employing prerecorded voice segments, has demonstrated positive payback in many customer service applications. The VRU's prerecorded, menu response design, which is interactive only in a very limited sense, is a precursor to full speech based on computer interaction. Its emergence depends on the pace of development in natural language processing algorithms.

While these advances are already beginning to enhance customer service applications, the big impact will come from the ability to observe and record people's behavior more comprehensively. This will allow automated systems to respond much more naturally and will allow much more fine-grained analysis of what people like and do not like in advertising, sales, and service applications. The resulting data can make such applications more efficient, effective, and appealing for users. Cultivating a rich accumulation of data describing interactions with customers and suppliers and capturing the interaction among employees should provide sustainable advantages. Customers will learn and adapt to the business interfaces of their suppliers, which we already know deters switching. Suppliers who use customer data to rapidly improve their offerings can establish a sustainable competitive position by using the information to plan future offerings. Competitors might be able to imitate these offerings, but they will nonetheless be at a disadvantage in anticipating and responding to future and rapidly deployed initiatives.

Collaboration/Enablement

Collaboration, which occurs when two or more people participate in a business task that relies on the use of common information, has broken the time and place barrier, thanks to communications technologies in many different formats. Collaboration has expanded from activities confined to a few participants within the same enterprise at the same location to collaborative activities involving many participants in many different locations, including outside participants such as suppliers and partners.[18] The tools are many, varied, and still emerging for collaboration. Some are better suited to computer-based augmentation than others. Those that are enablers of significant productivity gains also are indicators of where collaboration may be headed in the future: application sharing; whiteboards; Internet meetings, videoconferencing, and telephony; and collaborative groupware.

Application Sharing. Using PCs collaboratively to compose documents and presentations, financial reports, and project plans has become commonplace as the software supporting such tasks has become more functional and easier to use. A project plan imbedded in e-mail and shipped back and forth between two team partners is a poor substitute for what they really want to do—work on the plan at the same time. Application sharing helps by enabling two or more people to work together simultaneously via a network connection to their PCs.

Of course, this by itself is not sufficient. The collaborators also must be able to point out areas of the screen, enter information through the keyboard, and accept mutually agreed-to changes to the work product. Application sharing technologies support these capabilities, too. Most important, participants must be able to talk to each other—either through normal or Internet-based telephony. Clearly, the greater the friendliness and usability of application sharing technologies, the more they are likely to spread.

Whiteboards. Best thought of as a sketch pad with a network connection, whiteboard software allows one user to draw pictures on his or her PC while the image is simultaneously transmitted to other users. When those same users are connected in a teleconference, they can use a whiteboard to compose drawings to accompany their dialogue in much the same way that they might in a conference room at an actual whiteboard. Whiteboards can be structured to allow recording, highlighting, and other special features to make them as productive as when people are working in the same room.

Internet Meetings, Videoconferencing, and Telephony. Systems are now available for support of telephony, teleconferencing, and videoconferencing from an appropriately equipped PC connected to the Internet. For telephony, a PC must have a sound card and speakers and microphone; for videoconferencing, a video camera is added. The result is a very low-cost alternative to dedicated video conference centers.[19] When combined with application-sharing support and whiteboards, these facilities have tremendous potential. People from around the world can work together by communicating through voice, pictures, and PC applications as if they were physically together in a meeting. As other technologies mature, such meetings will eventually be automatically recorded, indexed, filed, and analyzed, and they may ultimately be preferred over face-to-face meetings for some kinds of work.

Collaborative Groupware. While many different types of software can fall under the general title of groupware, this discussion focuses on collaborative groupware or teamrooms as systems that allow documents, presentations, references, and other work products to be filed in a database that is accessible to a team, usually organized for a particular project. Such systems are distinct from workflow systems, which define a set of steps to be followed and provide routing and tracking of routine work items in a standardized business process. Collaborative systems typically allow team members to post comments and carry on discussions regarding the work items and to create and file new items. Viewing and editing access to items can be controlled by user profile.

Besides the important benefit of saving travel costs and time, these systems make it feasible to include team members who could not participate otherwise. Since teamrooms automatically record the progress of the team, new members can join the team and familiarize themselves with past progress at their own pace and on their own time. Teamrooms also facilitate tapping specialized expertise.

New versions of such systems have extended the teamroom idea to the Internet. One example is Lotus' Instant Teamroom, which makes a teamroom accessible using a Web browser from anywhere the Internet reaches. This is a tremendous enabler for cross-enterprise teams, allowing teams to get to work as quickly as the members are selected and encouraging work products to be shared across enterprise boundaries. (Note, however, that these powerful capabilities also raise serious concerns about data and work product security and intellectual property ownership—issues with which the firm must deal.)

A significant advance in collaboration may emerge with the integration of network-based meeting systems with network-based teamrooms. This merging of technologies offers great potential because it is focused on the key knowledge-producing activities of the firm. By enabling people to communicate better, more easily, and more frequently, information technology can help them discover new patterns, trends, and causalities in the marketplace, while recording what the company already knows. This enriches the company's sustainable asset, its knowledge, as a source of competitive advantage. However, the benefit is still on the horizon, since at present these aids are being applied in limited fashion and are not integrated. When a network-based work environment makes all of these IT aids available simultaneously, participants will be able to make a greater contributions to a firm's knowledge base, and firms will increase their ability to capture the knowledge of their employees in a reusable form.

Advanced Processing

Beyond gathering data and enabling communication, computers are taking on the role of helping people understand and analyze increasing volumes of data. New scientific discoveries and advances in engineering are producing computing-based tools that help people discover complex patterns in data. Such tools enable computers to process text and analyze content on a much higher level of interpretation than ever before and to continuously learn and adapt to the tasks they are asked to perform.

The advances have depended on tremendous increases in hardware computing power. But the underlying breakthroughs reside in the insightful ways that researchers and scientists have explored how people perform tasks and the tremendously creative ways in which they are enabling computers to accomplish these same tasks. This is particularly apparent in natural language understanding, data mining, and profiling and personalization as harbingers of future developments. All of these technological advances offer significant advantages to firms, particularly in the area of productivity. They are also changing the norms for business interaction. Other technologies that are potentially as significant are on the horizon—and firms can start incorporating them into their strategies now.

Natural Language Understanding (NLU). After decades of research on voice recognition, IBM, along with many others in the field, has developed software products that add speech-to-text conversion and speech-to-command capabilities to desktop and laptop computers. These products are emerging as robust alternatives to keyboard-based input and as a productivity-boosting application.[20]

The underlying technology records and analyzes sound waves produced by the speaker's voice. Part of the process involves recognition of the sounds coming before and after the word in question and thereby deals with the rudiments of higher-level understanding of natural language. This puts researchers on the road to a great number of new applications with significant payoffs. Tools will emerge that enable computers to discover obfuscated patterns in word-based communication, opening whole new areas and techniques for people to learn. Advanced text processing applications will help us learn how to get computers to analyze more general forms of text. As computers are better able to do so, they will provide more powerful aids to people, initially as more sophisticated routers and filers and perhaps later as research assistants. (A growing number of references on NLU are available in print and on the Internet.[21])

Datamining. New developments in data analysis tools have produced powerful new capabilities to identify and understand patterns that would otherwise remain buried in numbers. Typically, when people analyze data they start with a pattern that they expect to see and then test the data with statistical techniques to verify or disprove their original hypothesis. This approach is deductive and works for testing relationships and causalities that are prejudged as appearing in the data. But what if someone is looking at data describing behaviors or phenomena that do not fall into a hypothesis or that he or she does not yet understand?

This issue has taken on growing significance as computers enable firms to acquire and accumulate mountains of data inexpensively. Most firms keep track of volumes of customer data—what a customer purchased, when, and what else the customer purchased at the same time. Firms track product promotions, new introductions, and product modifications over time. They can also track or purchase detailed demographic data on their customers and potential customers that may be further indicators of needs, requirements, or similar interests. The problem is not the availability of data, but of undigested quantities of data. Datamining and inductive approaches can find significant patterns that would otherwise go undetected.

Typically, a datamining project starts by integrating and identifying inconsistencies in the data using automated tools. Datamining tools then analyze the data by employing inductive, rather than deductive, techniques to identify patterns, thereby avoiding preconceptions.

This approach has produced stunning results. Consider a direct marketing program. Its costs will depend on preparation and mailing, its success on the rate of customer response. Suppose the firm could identify in advance the customers most likely to respond. What if the mailer could be designed with the targeted customer preferences in mind? What if the best timing could also be identified? These applications of datamining are being done in all major industries as business intelligence, with significant influence on both corporate strategy and marketing.

Datamining is used to do all of this and more. In a joint venture, Kodak and CPI analyzed the positive impact of Kodak's brand on the market acceptance of digital film processing services in pilot stores.[22] Bank of America identified instances in which a different set of products would better match customer needs. BoA chose to proactively notify its customers, saving them money, engendering customer loyalty, and probably eliminating competitive exposure.[23]

Firstar Bank was able to achieve a fourfold increase in its direct marketing response rate.[24] ShopKo was able to identify better ways to merchandise based on correlated product purchases as a defense against Wal-Mart, saving millions of dollars in the process.[25] Dairyworld Foods was able to justify an acquisition price to Nestlé Canada and close the deal earlier by using datamining techniques to show the value of its brands.[26] Merck-Medco identified target opportunities for reducing prescription drug costs as a service to its customers by investigating the most successful therapies among commonly prescribed alternatives.[27]

In all of these cases, a datamining approach found a pattern that had eluded the firms. Once identified, it helped to make a significant difference.

Having proven itself across many industries, datamining has created an impetus to data gathering and has opened the way to further applications and integration with other applications and processes. Because datamining creates learning from a firm's existing data, it develops closer and more loyal relationships with customers and stimulates learning about what kinds of data to track. Firms that aggressively pursue datamining as part of their overall business strategy generate first-mover advantages.

Profiling and Personalization (Adaptive Knowledge Presentation). It is commonplace on the Internet for Web site visitors to be identified through a login process or through a unique identifier placed in their computers. Once an individual user is identified, the Web site can record a variety of information about a user's interaction with the site (such as name, interests, and consumer preferences). When users return, the Web site can identify them, greet them by name, present a customized layout and selection of content, and even suggest additional content that is likely to be of interest to them based on common interests they may have with other users.

Profiling and personalization, therefore, have the potential to alter the way customers expect to be treated on the Internet. Once users have "trained" a Web site to their interests and needs, they have developed an efficient vehicle for their purposes. To lure these

Combining IT and Knowledge

In the following case study, a major commercial bank achieved a significant market advantage by combining the power of information technology with the knowledge of its staffers. This case is instructive in demonstrating what can happen in many other firms as well.

The bank had a problem with a segment of large investors who each maintained a set of accounts with the bank and were served by systems set up for them. One system recorded the daily transactions against each account: deposits and payments made by agents of the investors. For security purposes, this system was accessible only to the bank's staff. Another system accumulated summary information and detailed daily activity and was accessible to customers. Each day, the previous day's activity was reviewed by the bank's account administrators and posted manually to a notification system that was accessible to the customers and their agents. The administrators developed detailed understanding of the accounts and contacted investors about any unexpected activity and to get instructions. The administrator's role in analyzing and evaluating account activity was a highly valued aspect of the service provided.

At first, having administrators also perform the manual postings seemed like a good idea, since they had to review the activity anyway. If there was a problem or an error, the administrator would review it, correct it, or note it before posting. Over time, as the investing activity increased, the manual posting process gradually encroached on the business day, delaying the start of the customer's investment activity. On rare occasions, errors in transcription had occurred. While these errors would be corrected the following day, customers understandably complained about lost investment opportunities and the extra work of tracking.

So the bank added extra checking steps and auditing in the posting process. Eventually, the bank started to lose customers to competitors who could post activity faster, even though they did no analysis. The bank realized that its enhanced analysis services were valued by customers only if such services did not cost too much in trading time.

IBM consultants were asked to recommend and implement system and business process improvements. The new design had to work faster, reduce errors, and allow the administrators to focus on analysis. The consultants were not allowed to alter the transaction system or the notification systems because these were used by other customers, too.

The solution was to automate the posting process with a simple client-server-based design. Clients used PCs to access both systems and the new posting process eliminated all transcription errors. It also allowed the administrators to monitor and approve each posting transaction as it was executed. The overall posting process was reduced from two hours to less than thirty minutes, enabling the bank to open its notification systems ahead of the competition while maintaining the individualized analysis service.

This project underscored the role of computers and the role of knowledgeable staffers. The bank staffers were not removed from the process, but they no longer wasted their time on tasks that computers could do faster and more accurately. Customers were made aware of the choice between high-value analysis and low-value posting. In the end, the technology allowed the bank to offer even faster postings than the competition while preserving individualized service. In this case, the bank made millions and preserved an important customer base by employing IT for what it does best and letting people do what they do best—the success came in creating the appropriate combination.

customers away, a competing Web site must provide content that is so much better that it outweighs the efforts the user would have to put forth to "retrain" another site. Meanwhile, the current site can increase the level of personalization and provide better content for the user.

Even with this simplistic view of the underlying economic drivers (switching costs and benefits), one can see why sites such as MyYahoo, MyExcite, and MyNetscape appeared and enhanced the functionality of their sites. Even smaller and more specialized businesses, such as Garden Escape Inc., CDNow, and Amazon.com, among many others, offer personalization of one form or another on their sites.[28]

Connection/Distribution Applications

Technology is moving ahead in the way information is connected, secured, and standardized and in how information gathering and discovery are automated. The now familiar HTML (Hypertext Markup Language) has gone through many revisions and updates and has been functionally enhanced. It serves as a globally standardized way to publish documents that show text and graphics and that allow imbedded applications. HTML, together with the browsers that interpret and present HTML documents, has several noteworthy features that in combination have led to a very effective standard for networked publishing. Web documents incorporate text with a variety of formatting options, graphics, animation, video and audio, scripted data retrieval (CGI), and even imbedded applications (Java). In addition, HTML documents can include references to other documents and hypertext links, which can refer to documents anywhere within the World Wide Web.

The conduct of business on the Internet has added new purposes and uses. Shopping, for example, is in its early stages an information-gathering process, well served for many goods by HTML-based documents that now comprise virtually all Web-based product catalogs. However, as the number of items grows, comparing items in a catalog becomes cumbersome and inefficient with HTML. A tool could be built with the capability to scan arbitrarily formatted pages and present the Web shopper with a product comparison table. But given the software maintenance headache of keeping the table up-to-date, it would probably not be worth the effort.

There are other instances in which similar difficulties emerge. Businesses wishing to interchange data have to worry about whether recipients can interpret the formats. Transactions such as product orders, acknowledgments, and shipping notices all vary from firm to firm. Companies that conduct business using Electronic Data Interchange are familiar with the high costs of setup and maintenance of these systems.

What if there were a way to send and receive information that preserves the rich functionality and formatting of HTML and overcomes these problems? The answer is Extended Markup Language (XML), an emerging replacement for HTML. In XML, the preparer of a catalog page not only produces the content, but also defines the content. The price, description, and picture are included in the page and identified as such. With self-explanatory data, the initial programming effort for processing programs, such as a comparison shopping tool, is reduced and ongoing maintenance is minimized. As these kinds of applications become viable, XML still allows the formatting that computer users have come to know and upon which they rely.

XML-based formats also appeal to firms in promoting products. While resistance to competitive comparison can be expected, price leaders have a strong motivation to support XML and others will follow for fear of being left out of the comparison process. Other favorable factors will also be at work, including a need for comparison arising from an abundance of alternative features and suppliers. In addition, XML offers a more economical means to exchange transaction data—either on the Internet or even within current EDI networks. For virtually all new applications that require the exchange of data, XML's self-defining features make it an obvious choice. In cases in which inter-firm relationships are based on electronic information exchange, firms have assumed that these relationships would persist because of the high cost of recreating such links with alternative partners. By changing the economics, XML and the Internet can call this assumption into question and lead firms to establishing strategic alliances on the basis of true value and knowledge exchange rather than on the basis of communication costs.

The Outlook

In looking ahead, here are some factors at play as firms make decisions on technology investments and strategy. Any decisions are appropriately made with strings attached to the future:

- Standard information format (HTML, future XML) and hyperlinked structure make aggregation of information from multiple sources fast and inexpensive.

- Automated information handling enables greater customization of information presentation.
- Standard protocols for online access to information sources reduce the cost of information distribution.
- Online access to information at its sources makes it less expensive to publish up-to-date, time-sensitive information and a larger volume of information.
- Online interactivity enables information consumers to contribute feedback in real time, enriching information content.
- Online interactivity enables firms to elicit consumer preferences unobtrusively and to develop richer consumer profiling that leads to:
  -greater personalization of content presentation to match consumer interests;
  -targeted advertising aligned to consumer interests; and
  -aggregated market wants/needs data for product/service design and development.

Summary

In confronting the pace of change in information technology, effective managers take into account key variables in terms of the capabilities and core competencies of their firms, their vision and strategy, and the competition. The technology variables are immediacy, collaboration, information capture and retrieval, pattern recognition, and security. The overriding consideration of change requires continuous monitoring of what technology can do and how it can change the competitive position of all firms.

The technological advances described in this chapter represent a more fundamental reality than downsizing, automating, or developing employee skills. They are influencing the design of work processes that generate knowledge as the reliance on data and its byproduct—knowledge—increases. Meanwhile, information grows at a compounded rate of 40 percent or more, a rate that is itself increasing. In addition, increasing amounts of work are done at the speed of electricity, rather than at the pace of human behavior.

In the final chapter, we turn to the issue of how all the aspects discussed throughout this book, including the enabling role of technology, are linked to management and leadership to produce profitable results.

For Further Reading

Michael A. Cusumano and David B. Yoffie, *Competing on Internet Time* (New York: Free Press, 1998).

The cases of Microsoft and Netscape are discussed in terms of developing strategies that rely on IT.

Subrata Dasgupta, *Technology and Creativity* (New York: Oxford University Press, 1996).

This book examines the thought processes involved in innovation and invention and illuminates the complexities of applying technology.

Richard A. Goodman and Michael W. Lawless, *Technology and Strategy: Conceptual Models and Diagnostics* (New York: Oxford University Press, 1994).

Presents a framework for thinking about strategy that provides analysis of the advantages to be derived from appropriate application of technology. Includes an instructive set of examples.

David C. Moschella, *Waves of Power: The Dynamics of Global Technology Leadership, 1964-2010* (New York: AMACOM, 1997).

A leading IT industry expert gives a historical and contemporary perspective on how technology is evolving and on the implications for business.

Donald A. Norman, *The Invisible Computer* (Cambridge, MA: MIT Press, 1998).

Presents the case for computers in the near future to become more embedded in work and machines.

Part Five

MASTERING CHANGE

11

Leading
the Way

The critical roles of leaders:
designer, teacher, and steward.
—Peter Senge

*This chapter focuses on three issues: how the forces analyzed
in this book play out in transforming organizations, what guidelines enable firms to harness their power, and what kind of leaders are needed in this period of great change. Guidelines, rules
of the road, and IBM's experience round out the picture.*

In recognizing that the times, and therefore the rules of the
game, are changing, business leaders are exploring uncertain
territories of a different kind. Unlike traditional explorers, they
have boundless information. But they still share the same
uncertainty about unpredictable consequences. Marco Polo "discovered" China and India for Europeans during the Middle Ages,
Christopher Columbus linked the Old to the New World, while Lewis
and Clark hiked and canoed their way across North America. All
three gave their generations a glimpse of an expansive future and lit-
erally showed them the way to it.

These explorers, who had the option of staying home and avoiding the risks of exploration, had a choice and they chose to explore.

The lead writer of this chapter is James W. Cortada.

199

Executives today don't have the option of "staying home" (the status quo). They must explore new solutions and new opportunities in order for their enterprises to prosper. The good news is that these opportunities exist because we are entering a new age of commerce and style of business management, as has become increasingly obvious to management teams across all industries. As with all new ages, much of the old remains while the new stirs the pot, creating opportunities and risks. The transformation of work and business goes on because of the emergence of new or more effective technologies, rapid communications and transportation, and a growing ability to coordinate ever-larger amounts of activities faster. The challenge for leaders of enterprises, both public and private, is to thrive in such a period.

The challenge is formidable. It's hard enough to run a firm in stable times (if there is such a thing), but doing so is even more complex in turbulent periods. But this is what management faces today. This book has discussed how to explore new continents, sail to new worlds, and map whole continents of opportunities. Like the explorers of old, executives face the complex task of coordinating all the assets and resources of the enterprise in order to reach the firm's goal(s) successfully. Meanwhile, stockholders insist on growth, not settling for a profitable steady state. To deal with the challenges, the leaders of firms must move quickly into newly defined areas of opportunity, executing fast while coordinating many activities simultaneously. That's why a central theme of this book has been that the successful firms we have worked with and their leaders integrate a realistic view of their markets and capabilities with sound management of knowledge, a process-centric approach, and forward-looking applications of technology. Transformation is holistic; one part of the approach does not dominate over another.

The team writing this book would have felt it was delivering its message more accurately if you could have read all of the book's chapters simultaneously, the way leaders of successful firms today are working to bring about multiple changes simultaneously. Whereas chapters and books are written to be read from front to back, sequentially, we want the lessons of transformation to be applied concurrently, based on the experiences of the 1990s.

Creating Strategies

So what future does your firm need to stake out? The classic gap analysis would compare what you are today with what you want to be tomorrow. Doing this is basic, sound management. But once is not enough for this age of business leaders. We find that successful firms continuously perform the gap analysis between their current states and their desired futures. It is a central task of executive leadership to perform this gap analysis across the dimensions that have been the subject of this book: knowledge, process, and technology. These aspects must be examined within the context of the issues described in Chapters 1 and 2: globalization, rapid entry of new competitors, the changing nature of work, and market demands.

In looking ahead, leaders of firms can develop a view of the future that is specific and relevant to their enterprises. In doing so, our research and experience show three forces that are at work in any effective vision and its strategies:

- knowledge-based development and execution of strategies,
- process-centric management of work, and
- technology-driven strategies and tactics.

All three of these forces exist in firms today and can be leveraged for change and growth. All three need to be coordinated. Every day, the work that already goes on in a firm has to be managed effectively while firms move toward whatever future they are pursuing. These three forces constitute text and context for the role of leader and call for a brief review before identifying the role of leadership in transformation.

The Role of Knowledge

Increasingly, firms are integrating knowledge management into their work and leveraging competencies to influence organizational vision and strategies. This enables organizations and their leaders to operate with far greater confidence in making decisions and in setting directions than was the case during the Second Industrial Age. As the economy of the world grows—as it has essentially done for the past 5,000 years—expect to see in the next decade or two accelerated growth and higher standards of skills and education, knowledge, and competencies. The cycle shows no signs of abating. The introduction of telecommunications and various forms of computing over the past century continues to fuel the move to knowledge-based business strategies.

Our challenge is to keep up with the demand for tools and management techniques to leverage the trend. That is why, for example, many corporations have established knowledge institutes or formal competencies (IBM has both) and why every nation in North America and Western Europe has expanded higher educational facilities since World War II. More than academic credentialing with degrees or certification, the trend recognizes the value of insight that is organized in a formal way (using lessons from the Second Industrial Age).

The Shift to Process

From the mid-1990s onward, we have found that almost every client we've assisted, as well as every executive at our own firm, has shifted to a process-centric view of work. The leaders of these firms are organizing process-managed work in ways that allow the organization to make its daily work efficient, while applying a growing body of tools and techniques for altering work activities to respond to new market conditions. This approach has two basic effects that are crucial for the new era we are entering. First, it shifts responsibility for results to the logical sources of experience and knowledge in the firm—front-line employees—who can act quickly and consistently with corporate intent. Second, the approach enables firms to develop processes that create links with other firms, including suppliers and customers. As processes increasingly cross corporate boundaries (as in supply chains) to share communications infrastructures, mutually accessible databases, and employees, the ability to be compatible and linkable becomes essential.

A subtle third effect is emerging as well: namely, using process management as a way of thinking about how work gets done and providing a way of rationalizing and organizing activities. Looking ahead, process management will continue to develop and be refined as best practices are documented and shared across industries and inside firms. Not hype, this is a "down-in-the-trenches" approach that is practical, realistic, and effective.

The Impact of Technology

The most obvious feature of any organization's activities and those of society in developed nations is technology. If people a thousand years from now remember nothing else about progress in the 20th century, they will recall that it was the age in which the computer was invented and deployed. But, of course, there has been much more. This was the century in which electricity was fully deployed, along with the telephone. Many other technologies also came along to move information: radio, television, data communications, pagers, cell phones, personal data assistants, and so forth. Many technologies came into existence that users are now applying in new combinations. Even newer technologies from engineers and scientists in university and corporate labs will add to the flood of innovations. The momentum across all three fronts—new uses of technology by users, new products from IT vendors, and new base technologies—shows no signs of slowing. Indeed, the technology momentum is bound to increase because of its usefulness, value, and importance.

It is no surprise that technology providers became the fastest-growing (and in some cases the most valuable) firms within a nation's economy during the 1980s and 1990s. It is also no surprise that many firms emerging as highly successful at the end of the 1990s are not limited to new software startups (e.g., Netscape, Microsoft, or even Amazon.com). They also include companies that nobody would have thought were IT-based. Today, for example, General Motors, Lockheed, and American Airlines are massive users of computing. They have the internal capabilities (competencies) of going toe-to-toe in some of the traditional computer industries of the past (if they chose to). What they are doing is applying technology effectively to do what they want to do best: building and selling vehicles and aircraft or flying people around the world. In short, technology is too important to be limited to technology firms.

A solid understanding of the capabilities and implications of technology can help firms define massively large new markets to pursue, as it has done for so many corporations. At IBM, for example, it led to the creation of a new line of business—consulting services (called IBM Global Services)—that annually generates over $30 billion in revenue, adding nearly one-third more cash and profits than would have been thought possible a decade earlier! Even though the team that wrote this book works at IBM, its focus is not on technology but on transformation. That's why less than one-third of this book is about technology. Why? Because successful transformation—including IBM's—depends on a holistic approach in creating a new future.

Transformation Lessons

Leaders who have succeeded in transforming their organizations have demonstrated three elements of success. First, they have brought their employees along, which means buy-in for the change strategies to be implemented. Without employee support, nothing happens, or very little. Second, a realistic approach calls for a combination of various short- and long-term approaches that are simultaneously employed and applied at various speeds and forms throughout the organization. This means that some processes are incrementally improved over time, while others are scrapped or reengineered. Some individuals will use the Internet to conduct business, while others will rely on relatively unchanging centralized computer applications. It means that new skills are needed along with improvement of pre-existing ones. Third, the community of managers, employees, business partners, customers, and government regulators all have learned how to apply basic "rules of the road" concerning constant innovation.

Sound soft? Well, the change gurus have universally come to the conclusion that the soft issues are really the hard issues in transformation. IBM's own change management experts rarely deal with such hard issues as financial incentives and performance plans. Instead, they're asked to work on the development of communications processes to help persuade employees to embrace change, on measurements of progress, and on processes that lead to enhanced use of skills and intellectual capital. A decade ago, these experts worked on very different issues, all hard, all measurable, and all directly coupled to the performance—and not the processes—of organizations. In succeeding, the leadership in transformation:

- Sets priorities in the allocation of such resources as people, budgets, and facilities. It also establishes more comprehensive measurement systems to replace those used during the Industrial Age. These new metrics focus on how people perform in an environment that rewards those who are able and willing to keep priorities flexible.

- Coordinates knowledge management, process implementation, and technology in a synergistic way so that they complement each other, while allowing the organization to change rapidly and develop insights in implementing change.

- Reaches out via partnerships, mergers, takeovers, and expansion. As globalization moves from rhetoric to reality, executives can no longer think of the firm as a company with clearly defined borders. The boundaries of enterprises are becoming porous for good reason. A firm needs skills and assets coming and going all the time. If there is one managerial competency that we find executives lack, it is the ability to implement mergers, acquisitions, and alliances and to capitalize on outreach. This is a skill that, in the next few years, will make or break many firms, as linking processes, knowledge management, and technology determines the fortunes of an enterprise.

The Crucial Role of Leadership

Talk to any CEO or senior executive who has implemented the kinds of changes discussed in this book and you typically hear two things: "It was the most exciting period of my business career" and "It was the hardest thing I ever had to do." They all will also say that without their personal leadership, change would not get done. This is not ego at work. It reflects what employees in many surveys have reported. Change is hard, not simply because people resist it, but because it is not always clear what and how to change—the reason for writing this book—and out of fear that change will hurt personal careers and the fortunes of the firm.

Pushing any organization into a state of continuous change is hard to do. Leaders confront this problem in such firms as IBM, 3M, and ABB or in firms changing whole divisions for the first time for compelling reasons—as occurred at Xerox or at high-tech agribusinesses (such as Monsanto) or in pharmaceuticals because of the emergence of genetically based medications. These companies are highly respected, recognized by competitors as having effective leadership and motivated employees. Yet they, too, find change hard. In the final analysis, if anything remotely resembles a "silver bullet," it is management not hidebound by tradition and leadership displayed at all levels of the organization.

When companies that were in trouble in the early 1990s—such as Xerox, Ford, and IBM—crafted successful transformation strategies, they all did one thing in common: their leadership looked at the realities of the marketplace, selected a view of that world, and crafted strategies to exploit the situation to the advantage of their firms. It did not matter whether they were exactly right They formed a view of the world and acted as if it were true. In hindsight, the successful ones were correct because they either "got it right" or built a future in the image they had created. What they had faced was more than a challenge; they had confronted a profound threat to their profitability, even their survival.

In the case of Xerox, Japanese competitors were selling copiers for less than it cost Xerox to make them. In Ford's situation, foreign manufacturers were making higher-quality cars that were more fuel-efficient and less expensive. In IBM's case, the problem was a fundamental shift to new products and services that were not fully in its quiver. In each instance, the dynamics of existing business practices had to change.

These views led to new strategies, which led to new transformation activities concerning the application of process management, institutionally held knowledge, competencies, and technologies. In the example of IBM, when Louis Gerstner came into the firm as CEO, he soon concluded with the IBMers already there that the company understood correctly the business realities it faced. He also came to the conclusion that execution of existing strategies needed some modification and, more important, that those strategies needed to be implemented rapidly. This called for a wide variety of changes, ranging from a new emphasis on certain products and services to reorganizations, and from tactical steps to getting the firm back into a profitable state to bringing in fresh talent. In moving ahead, Gerstner had to commit the firm to a view of the world that matched what had to be done. Gerstner did this by saying that the future for IBM lay in a networked world, one filled with PCs, the Internet, and business-to-business electronic commerce. It would be a world in which IBM had to advise its customers on how to reach the new age, often doing the nuts-and-bolts technical work for them, which represented a major shift in emphasis for a company that had spent eighty years being a world-class manufacturing firm.

Gerstner could have picked a different view of the world, but he didn't. That was it. Several years later, after much reengineering of the activities and offerings of the firm, IBM found itself very much at the center of the emerging networked world. By having picked the "right" future, IBM was able to expand profitably in the second half of the 1990s, in ways unthinkable in the early 1990s. By the end of the 1990s, one-third of IBM's business consisted of consulting and services (IBM Global Services). Big computer systems (mainframes), while very important in a networked world, ended up providing the smallest share of IBM revenues since the early 1960s. By picking a future and focusing the resources of the firm to help make it a reality, Gerstner succeeded.

It is the same story for Xerox, Ford, ABB, Phillips, and so many other companies. It is even a tale of governments, most notably the United States and the embryonic government called the European Union. All are forward-looking, all stake out a view of the future and commit their resources to it, and all are staying the course.

Above all, the experience of the 1990s has highlighted the difference between just managing and really leading in a time of continuous change that calls for different ways of managing the assets of an organization. Management has traditionally focused on maintaining the status quo. Managers have always been taught to get things done with the resources at hand (and have been rewarded for doing so) against a predictable set of targets, often under the assumption that they operated in a relatively stable business environment. That requirement does not go away in any firm experiencing change. But doing business as usual loses primacy. Only maintaining the status quo is deadly during this period of great change. Defending the status

The Role of Leadership

Because leadership can make the difference between success and failure in transformation, the thinking and actions of company leaders stand out as guidelines to implementing and maintaining change. Here is how, in a company-wide memo to IBM's management team, Lou Gerstner, Chairman and CEO of IBM, characterized the role of leadership in IBM's matrixed environment:

> There is no long-term, sustainable competitive advantage in technology. At any given time, some competitor's nose will be in front of the pack with a faster server, a more powerful database or networking product. I'm not minimizing the importance of technology leadership. Every company must fight and invest to stay ahead. But no company can maintain, year-in, year-out, a marketplace advantage on technology alone. However, when it comes to integration, at IBM we've got a big lead on everyone else, a lead we should be able to sustain, and even lengthen.
>
> There's no doubt a matrixed environment makes our jobs as managers and leaders much more challenging. It also makes them more important. While a badly managed matrix can be worse than a hierarchy—in being both rigid and confusing—a well-managed matrix is highly fluid and adaptable. Roles change often. Teams form and disband. Decisions about which business will lead in any particular situation are not codified. This puts a premium on the judgment of leaders at every level. You decide which opportunities offer the highest potential return. You decide where to deploy our people, capital, and time.

This memo, five years into Gerstner's tenure as Chairman and CEO, illustrates the need to reaffirm and reinforce collaboration and teaming. After citing examples of how the approach has produced results, Gerstner emphasized his position and his policy:

> I can only reach one conclusion. If something is a strength in one situation and a weakness in another, then there's not an endemic problem. We don't need to fix the system

> (though we'll continue to improve things like cross-company processes and the measurement system). What we need are leaders with the right attitude.
>
> For example, if we have staff people who think their job is to monitor line people and turn them in when they do something wrong, no management system is going to succeed. But if our staff people have an attitude that says, "My job is to ensure that all the capability of this company is channeled to the person at the point of contact with the customer. I'm here to help them win business"—then the matrix becomes an asset because we're using it to deliver IBM value to the marketplace.

quo too aggressively in the face of the need for change is what got so many firms into hot water in the 1980s and early 1990s, and it is what got the economies of Russia, especially Japan, and many other nations into deep trouble in the late 1990s. In short, resisting change can be very dangerous to the bottom line. Successful firms have managed to walk the fine line of maintaining responsible controls over their assets while simultaneously transforming to meet new market conditions. It is leadership that enables firms to walk this fine line.

Leadership today is all about coping with change, of being ahead of the curve. In a transforming company, what is leadership like? Our experience with clients and our own company's leadership practices call attention to five patterns of behavior, particularly in large, complex firms:

1. Leaders are innovators. Leaders are present at all levels of an organization, not just at the top. They can be process leaders constantly improving their small world of responsibility. Often, they are middle- and divisional-level executives dealing with the realities of changing market conditions. When a corporation is in trouble, effective leadership comes from the chairman. Wherever they are, leaders challenge existing way of doing things, often experimenting and usually moving forward incrementally. These are the people academics and business writers all point to as individuals who often behave differently and who avoid narcissistic organizational politics. When they do "play politics" within their organizations, they do so to get results. The lower in the organization they are, the more likely they are to tinker with processes. The higher they are in the enterprise, the more they leverage budgets, organization, and rhetoric.

2. Leaders get involved personally. Leaders go beyond simply crafting a vision or settling on a strategy. They personally invest time in the transformation initiative. They work the phones, get involved in meetings where work is being done, and walk the floor encouraging employees to stay the course. The key is personal investment of time while contributing personally to the discussions and decisions being made. Simply putting a vision "out there" and asking others to do all the work is a formula for failure. Leaders participate in the work of transformation, wherever they are in the organization. Gross generalizations, yes, but our message is clear: Leaders personally do the work of transformation, regardless of where they are perched in the organization.

3. Leaders know what needs to get done in general, though not in detail. The details emerge during implementation. Typically, transformation begins with someone concluding that "we have to change things around here." It may be as simple as that, before leading to an analysis of what has to change, why, and how. We notice in almost every instance that the definition of what to change and how evolves during the act of transformation as the leadership gets a better idea of what the problems are and where the organization needs to go. The act of implementing a transformation strategy leads to the specific actions that result in desired changes. That's why it is often so difficult for executives to settle on a hard-and-fast timetable for transformation or for consultants to pin down clients on exactly what they want. As knowledge experts point out, the process of transformation transforms our own thinking as we get feedback and do the work.

4. Leaders can deal with ambiguity and risk. Given the uncertainties of change, dealing with ambiguity and risk is a job requirement for transformation leaders, since most transformations produce unanticipated consequences (both positive and negative). Nonetheless, innovative leaders have a sense of the direction they are going, the ability to persuade others to come along (the cheerleading role so many students of leadership talk about), and the confidence that they can deal with what-ever problems pop up along the way. This confidence is bred either into the leader or, more often today, is taught and reinforced. Mistakes aris-ing from experimentation are tolerated, successful innovations are rewarded, and tools and techniques for transformation are taught (the subject of this book). The key is not to fear change, but rather to have confidence that whatever arises can be handled with the assistance of the many knowledgeable people available inside and outside the organ-ization.

5. Leaders understand how much their organizations can change and at what speed. Change experts warn that too much change too fast or change that is too slow or not enough can weaken or destroy any transformation initiative. Leaders often have an instinct for the appropriate rate and quantity of change. Today, they have many formal tools and techniques to monitor the process of change, and they can also call on knowledgeable consultants to conduct a formal assessment of how participants feel about changes and why. The leaders factor these attitudes into the design and implementation of plans for trans-formation initiatives, realizing that ignoring them is the single leading cause of failed innovations.

Other potential causes of failure vary widely and include:

- failing to clearly establish objectives and measurable goals;
- insufficient effort in "selling" proposed innovations to employees, business partners, and customers; and
- failing to eliminate personal incentives for resisting change.

Leadership in a transforming organization is about managing the "soft" issues of corporate culture and human behavior, whether it is building a culture of innovation at 3M or one that is highly entrepre-neurial at ABB or project-based cultures in the Silicon Valley. The point is that institutional culture varies enormously, depending on the nature and goals of the organization.

Corporate culture itself is a fascinating topic that is of crucial inter-est to innovative leaders because the culture is, in and of itself, a com-petency—a capacity of the organization. If people routinely are com-fortable in launching marketing initiatives, as we see, for instance, at IBM, a competency emerges that facilitates transformation. If an organization respects personal knowledge and skill, as at the Lucent Corporation (formally Bell Labs) or at IBM's Watson Laboratory, people are willing to experiment with new forms of technology and apply them in novel business ways.

There is a growing body of knowledge developing about how to identify and change corporate culture. The culture issue now affects the vast majority of IBM's consulting engagements because a firm cannot innovate successfully without a good cultural match. Firms also realize that policies, practices, and processes need to evolve simultaneously with the more obvious ecological or marketing changes. The good news is that transforming organizations can turn to best practices, which are rapidly being collected. Tools to analyze corporate cultures are also widely available. The risk of "getting it wrong" is declining as an increasing number of organizations implement a constant flow of innovations and as consultants and academics collect "war stories" and develop techniques for transformation.

Summary

A new business ecology has emerged whose metaphors are biological, not mechanical. It involves thinking in terms of the evolution of a species, not the fine workings of a machine. As we move away from a period of relative business stability into a new age of change and instability (the biological metaphor at work), the fit, the lucky, and the adaptive will survive and thrive. The weak and unlucky (or, to use biological ideas, those who cannot evolve) shrivel and die.

In a world that is global and networked, successful firms are technically savvy and they are willing and able to change and adapt. This account of how to change is very different from what any of us would have written in the early 1990s. So much has changed, so many management teams have learned new things. How best, then, should we "net it out"? What message should we leave you with? You know change is continuous but that it can be constantly managed. You know that strategies for transformation have become a subfield of management practices—a subfield with its own disciplines, tools, and techniques.

We think the final message, one that captures the spirit of what needs to be done, was provided by British playwright George Bernard Shaw at the dawn of the20th century:

> People are always blaming their circumstances for what they are. I don't believe in circumstances. The people who get on in the world are the people who get up and look for the circumstances they want and if they don't find them, make them.

Notes

Chapter 1

1. Stephen E. Ambrose, *Undaunted Courage* (New York: Touchstone Book, New York, 1996), p. 69.

2. At the same time as reengineering has faced criticism, discussions have gone on about its appropriate uses. See, for example, Joseph N. Kelada, "Is Reengineering Replacing Total Quality?" *Quality Progress*, December 1994.

3. Ambrose, *op.cit.*, p. 70.

4. For a historical view of technology and change, see Edward Tenner, *Why Things Bite Back: Technology and the Revenge of Unintended Consequences* (New York: Alfred Knopf, 1997).

5. William J. Baumol, Sue Anne Batey Blackman, and Edward N. Wolff, *Productivity and American Leadership: The Long View* (Cambridge, MA: MIT Press, 1989), pp. 251-287. For an overview of various economic views, see Thomas K. Landauer, *The Trouble with Computers* (Cambridge, MA: MIT Press, 1995), pp. 1-46.

6. More exciting than Kearns' statement is the story behind Xerox's transformation, in David T. Kearns and David A. Nadler, *Prophets in the Dark: How Xerox Reinvented Itself and Beat Back the Japanese* (New York: Harper-Business, 1992).

7. The best account of this issue is provided by Frederick F. Reichheld and Thomas Teal, *The Loyalty Effect: The Hidden Force Behind Growth, Profits, and Lasting Value* (Boston: Harvard Business School Press, 1996).

8. Michael Hammer and James Champy, *Reengineering the Corporation* (New York: HarperBusiness, 1993); W. Edwards Deming, *Out of the Crisis*,

2nd ed. (Cambridge, MA: MIT Center for Advanced Engineering Study, 1986); Joseph M. Juran, *Juran on Leadership and Quality: An Executive Handbook* (New York: Free Press, 1989).

9. Charles Handy, *The Age of Uncertainty* (Boston: Harvard Business School Press, 1989) is perhaps the best known of his statements.

10. Thomas D. Kuczmarski, *Innovation: Leadership Strategies for the Competitive Edge* (Lincolnwood, IL: American Marketing Association and NTC Business Books, 1996), pp. 125-156; Steven L. Goldman, Roger N. Nagel, and Kenneth Preiss, *Agile Competitors and Virtual Organizations: Strategies for Enriching the Customer* (New York: Van Nostrand Reinhold, 1995), pp. 16, 24, 76.

11. James W. Cortada, *Best Practices in Information Technology: How Corporations Get the Most Value from Exploiting Their Digital Investments* (Englewood Cliffs, NJ: Prentice Hall, 1998).

Chapter 2

1. This theme is well-explored by James F. Moore, *The Death of Competition: Leadership and Strategy in the Age of Business Ecosystems* (New York: HarperBusiness, 1996) and by Carl Shapiro and Hal R. Varian, *Information Rules: A Strategic Guide to the Network Economy* (Boston: Harvard Business School Press, 1999).

2. While most of these studies, which are used by IBM consultants to assist their clients, remain unpublished, one has been published and includes findings from the other studies: *Global Insurance to the Twenty-First Century* (White Plains, NY, IBM Corporation, 1996).

3. James W. Cortada, *Managing in the Information Age* (forthcoming).

4. Recently explained by two outstanding historians: David S. Landes, *The Wealth and Poverty of Nations* (New York: W.W. Norton, 1998), pp. 463-524; David Hacket Fischer, *The Great Wave: Price Revolutions and the Rhythm of History* (New York: Oxford University Press, 1996), pp. 203-234.

5. See Fischer, *The Great Wave*.

6. Technologies have profoundly influenced this, as they do today. Ester Boserup, *Population and Technological Change: A Study of Long-Term Trends* (Chicago: University of Chicago Press, 1981), pp. 3-7.

7. Alan Stone, *How America Got On-Line* (Armonk, NY: M.E. Sharpe, 1997), p. 195.

8. IBM Consulting Group and The Economist Intelligence Unit, *Global Communications to the Year 2000* (New York: Economist Intelligence Unit, 1996), p. 9.

9. Franklin R. Edwards, *The New Finance* (Washington, D.C.: AEI Press, 1996), pp. 114-115.

10. For a look at the issues, see David C. Mowery and Nathan Rosenberg, *Paths of Innovation: Technological Change in 20th Century America* (Cambridge: Cambridge University Press, 1998).

11. IBM Corporation, *Annual Reports* (1980-1999).

Chapter 3

1. Jerry Bowles and Joshua Hammond, *Beyond Quality: How 50 Winning Companies Use Continuous Improvement* (New York: G.P. Putnam's Sons, 1991), pp. 147-151.

2. Abraham Maslow's Hierarchy of Needs has five levels: Level 1, Physiological; Level 2, Safety; Level 3, Affiliation; Level 4, Esteem; Level 5, Self-Actualization. See Abraham Maslow, *Motivation and Personality* (New York: Harper & Row, 1954).

3. Research on the metrics involved has begun. See, for example, G. Bennett Stewart's pioneering book, *The Quest for Value: The EVA Management Guide* (New York: HarperBusiness, 1991), and, more recently, Alan S. Cleland and Albert V. Bruno, *The Market Value Process: Bridging Customer and Shareholder Value* (San Francisco: Jossey-Bass, 1996).

4. As applied in e-business with the sale of information and services. See Carl Shapiro and Hal R. Varian, *Information Rules: A Strategic Guide to the Network Economy* (Boston: Harvard Business School Press, 1999), pp. 53-81.

5. The CEO of Lotus Development Corporation describes these e-business implications in Jeff Papows, *Enterprise.com: Market Leadership in the Information Age* (Reading, MA: Perseus Books, 1998), pp. 87-104.

6. IBM routinely uses CVM techniques to link its activities to what makes sense to customers. The approach enhances the firm's ability to make products attractive, such as the AS/400 and the entire line of laptop PCs.

7. For case studies, see David B. Yoffie (ed.), *Competing in the Age of Digital Convergence* (Boston: Harvard Business School Press, 1997).

8. Sense-and-respond issues frequently emerge here and in the ongoing management of CVM. For more, see IBM's research and experiences in Steve

H. Haeckel, *Adaptive Enterprise: Creating and Leading Sense-and-Respond Organizations* (Boston: Harvard Business School Press, 1999).

9. IBM consultants began observing the criticality of alignment across all these parts of a business in the early 1990s. For a discussion of the issues involved, as related, for example, to IT, see the series of articles on alignment in Jerry N. Luftman (ed.), *Competing in the Information Age* (New York: Oxford University Press, 1996).

Chapter 4

1. For an analysis of what's forcing a focus on knowledge, see "Introduction to Knowledge in Organizations," in *Knowledge in Organizations*, Laurence Prusak, ed. (Boston: Butterworth-Heinemann, 1997), pp. ix-xv.

2. Cited in Thomas H. Davenport and Laurence Prusak, *Working Knowledge: How Organizations Manage What They Know* (Cambridge, MA: Harvard University Press, 1997), p. xii.

3. *Ibid*, p. 5.

4. For a fuller discussion, see Davenport and Prusak, *op. cit.* pp. 1-19.

5. See Charles Perrow, *Normal Accidents* (New York: W.W. Norton, 1989) for an extensive analysis of this phenomenon.

6. Polly LaBarre, "People Go, Knowledge Stays," *Fast Company*, September 1998, p. 48.

7. Shoshana Zuboff, "Technologies That Informate," in *Human Resource Management: Trends and Challenges*, Richard Walton and Paul Lawrence, eds. (Cambridge, MA: Harvard Business School Press, 1985).

8. Steven E. Prokesch, "Unleashing the Power of Learning: An Interview with British Petroleum's John Browne," *Harvard Business Review*, 75, September/October 1997, p. 6.

9. Chuck Salter, "This Company's Seen the Future of Customer Service," *Fast Company*, February/March 1998, pp. 34, 36.

10. "Managing Corporate Communications in the Information Age," Institute for the Future, Menlo Park, CA. Survey conducted during August and September 1996.

11. Davenport and Prusak, *Working Knowledge*, p. x.

Chapter 5

1. In featuring the Scotchgard™ example and the statement by former 3M president William L. McKnight, the 3M home page states: "Since our beginnings at the turn of the century, 3M's success has come from producing innovative solutions to our customers' problems."

2. IBM's intellectual capital system and use of technology to support it is thoroughly explained by Kuan-Tsae Huang, "Capitalizing on Intellectual Assets," *IBM Systems Journal*, Vol. 37, No. 4, 1998, pp. 570-583.

3. Peter Murray and Andrew Myers, *Information Strategy*, September 1997, p. 33.

4. See Thomas A. Stewart, "The Cunning Plots of Leadership," *Fortune*, September 7, l998, pp. 165-166.

5. Michael Lewis, *Liar's Poker* (New York: Penguin Books, 1990), p. 48.

6. For a fuller treatment of this issue, see Liam Fahey and Laurence Prusak, "The Eleven Deadliest Sins of Knowledge Management," *California Management Review*, Vol. 40, No. 3, Spring 1998, pp. 265-276.

7. Lou Gerstner, March 19, 1998, CeBIT 98 conference keynote address.

Chapter 6

1. For a description of IBM's consulting competencies in the late 1990s, see IBM Corporation, *Transformation Consulting Services: Thinking Beyond the Next Wave* (White Plains, NY: IBM Corporation, 1998), Order Number G310-0725-00.

Chapter 7

1. For a discussion of matrix management, see Erik.W. Larson and David H. Gobeli, "Matrix Management: Contradictions and Insights," *California Management Review*, Vol. 29, No. 4, Summer 1987.

2. Jenny C. McCune, "Building an E-business Infrastructure," *Beyond Computing*, September 1998, p. 31.

3. Dennis Bengston and Eric Lesser, "Turbocharging Business Processes with Knowledge," *Journal of Innovative Management*, Vol. 4, No. 1, Fall 1998, pp. 13-22.

4. "Process Classification Framework: Overview," prepared by the International Benchmarking Clearinghouse of the American Productivity & Quality Center (APQC), Houston, Texas, in partnership with Arthur Andersen & Co.

5. For a summary of the benefits of process-centric management, see Michael Hammer, "The Process Organization: An Executive Perspective," Hammer and Company, April 1998, www.hammerandco.com.

6. Michael Hammer and James Champy, *Reengineering the Corporation* (New York: HarperBusiness, 1993), pp. 108-109.

7. Warren Bennis and Patricia Ward Biederman, *Organizing Genius* (Reading, MA: Addison-Wesley Publishing Company, 1996), p. 3.

8. James L. Creighton and James W. R. Adams, *CyberMeeting* (New York: AMACOM, 1998), pp. 181, 164.

Chapter 8

1. Michael Hammer and James Champy, *Reengineering the Corporation* (New York: HarperBusiness, 1993), pp. 32-35.

2. Michael Hammer, "The Process Organization: An Executive Perspective," Hammer and Company, April 1998, www.hammerandco.com.

3. Robert S. Kaplan and David P. Norton, *Balanced Scorecard* (Boston: Harvard Business School Press, 1996), pp. 47-62.

4. His remarks were made repeatedly during the 1990s and can be found in his annual reports, and press interviews with all key business magazines of the period.

Chapter 9

1. Widely quoted in the press, with interviews in such American journals as *Fortune* and *BusinessWeek*. His comments were also coupled to an aggressive advertising campaign to introduce new services throughout the late 1990s.

2. Figures reported by Travelocity.com, ITN.com, and Travelweb.com.

3. Microsoft three-year strategy memo, quoted by *The Wall Street Journal*, June 5, 1997.

4. USTAR reported 1996 registration of about 36,000 on its Web site, at www.ustar.com. In December 1997, CMPnet (www.cmpnet.com) reported a six percent decline in U.S. travel agents and the number of agents at 32,000.

5. See Thomas Hoffman, "AI-based Software Models Help Cut Production Costs," *Computerworld*, September 2, 1996, pp. 59-60.

6. Erik Brynjolfsson and Lorin Hitt, "Paradox Lost? Firm-Level Evidence of High Returns to Information Systems Spending," *Management Science*, April 1996, pp. 541-558. A representative summary of the controversy appears in Daniel E. Sichel, *The Computer Revolution: An Economic Perspective* (Washington, DC: Brookings Institution, 1997), pp. 1-14, 32-36.

7. Marilyn M. Parker, *Strategic Information and Information Technology* (Upper Saddle River, NJ: Prentice Hall, 1996), pp. 141-163; Richard A. Goodman and Michael W. Lawless, *Technology and Strategy: Conceptual Models and Diagnostics* (New York: Oxford University Press, 1994), pp. 51-160; Subrata Dasgupta, *Technology and Creativity* (New York: Oxford University Press, 1996), p. 8; Thomas H. Davenport, *Information Ecology* (New York: Oxford University Press, 1997), pp. 179-180.

8. See, for example, Thomas H. Davenport, *Process Innovation: Reengineering Work Through Information Technology* (Boston: Harvard Business School Press, 1993) or Don Tapscott and Art Caston, *Paradigm Shift: The New Promise of Information Technology* (New York: McGraw-Hill, 1993).

9. These issues are explored by Thomas H. Davenport and Lawrence Prusak, *Working Knowledge: How Organizations Manage What They Know* (Boston: Harvard Business School Press, 1997).

10. IBM Corporation, *Transformation Consulting Services* (North Tarrytown, NY: IBM Corporation, 1997). Order Number G310-0725-00.

11. In this discussion, we favor Michael Porter's view of strategy as comprising distinctive capabilities. See "What Is Strategy?" *Harvard Business Review*, November/December 1996, pp. 61-78.

12. Southwest Airlines Web site, www.iflyswa.com, June 1998.

13. Michael E. Porter, *Competitive Advantage: Creating and Sustaining Superior Performance* (New York: Free Press, 1985), pp. 26-61.

14. The main point of research by Alfred D. Chandler, *Paths of Learning* (New York: The Free Press, forthcoming).

Chapter 10

1. For a discussion of the types of changes and implications for management, see Michael Albrecht and James W. Cortada, "Optimizing Investments in Information Technology" *National Productivity Review*, Summer 1998, pp. 53-60.

2. IBM Consulting Group, "IT Transformation Benchmark Consortium Report," November 1993, pp. 3-19.

3. Earl and David F. Feeny, "Is Your CIO Adding Value?" *Sloan Management Review*, Spring 1994, p. 12.

4. Wanda J. Orlikowski and Debra C. Gash, "Changing Frames: Understanding Technological Change in Organizations," Alfred P. Sloan School of Management Working Paper WP #3368-92.

5. Thomas C. Powell and Anne Dent-Micallef, "Information Technology as Com-petitive Advantage: The Role of Human, Business, and Technology Resources" *Strategic Management Journal*, Vol. 18, No. 5 1997, pp. 375-405.

6. "Shorter Circuits," *IBM Research*, No. 3, 1998, pp. 10-15.

7. Interview with a lead architect and project leader in IBM's Internet applications development team. Productivity boosts over C++ and other languages are due to clearer language syntax, automation in code documentation, code reuse, automated garbage collection, and readily available class libraries.

8. A new generation of software in ERP, for example, is pointing the way. Acceptance has been widespread, with vendors experiencing double-digit growth rates since 1970.

9. In 1996, IBM became the first IT vendor to introduce voice recognition software, which operated in a PC for word processing. Today, several versions later, it performs more than dictation and data entry. The tools are called Via Voice™ 98.

10. Tombo Inoue, Kenichi Okada, and Yutaka Matsushita, "How Can Feelings Be Conveyed in a Network? Use of Gestural Animations as Nonverbal Information." *Symbiosis of Human Artifact: Proceedings of the Sixth International Conference on Human Computer Interactions* (HCI International 1995), Vol. A, pp. 23-28.

11. See the study mentioned in "More Than Words Can Say," *American Salesman*, Vol. 14, No. 4, pp. 24-26.

12. See "The Human Centered Interface," *IBM Research*, Nos. 1 and 2, 1998, pp. 16-20.

13. Roger A. Lindau, "Automatic Data Capture and Its Impact on Productivity," *International Journal of Production Economics*, Vol. 52, Nos. 1 and 2, pp. 91-103.

14. See "Putting Pen to Smart Paper" *IBM Research*, No. 3, 1997, pp. 12-14; and "The Pen is Mightier...," *IBM Research*, Nos. 3 and 4, 1995, p. 35.

15. See "Recognizing Forms," *IBM Research*, Nos. 3 and 4, 1995, p. 33.

16. See "Is It Live or Is It Text to Speech?" *IBM Research*, No. 3, 1998, p. 5.

17. Sharon L. Oviatt and Phillip R. Cohen, "The Contributing Influence of Speech and Interaction in Human Discourse Patterns." In *Intelligent User Interfaces*, Joseph W. Sullivan and Sherman W. Tyler, eds. (New York: ACM Press, 1991), pp. 76-77.

18. This overview of collaboration is based on IBM's Collaboration Blueprint describing the Collaboration Resource Manager. See www.software.ibm.com /openblue/id1g1/2_1.htm.

19. Most PCs come equipped for sound already. A microphone costs less than $20. A PC color video camera costs about $200.

20. See "Is It Live or Is It Text to Speech?" *IBM Research*, No. 3, 1998, p. 5.

21. See www.cs.curtin.edu.au/ ~ roger/thesis_html/node12.html for an NLU mistake overview and print references. See mu.www.media.mit. edu/#demos for demonstration of technologies produced by the MIT Media Lab.

22. Deborah Ashbrand, "Is Datamining Ready for the Masses?" *Datamation*, November 1997, pp. 66-71.

23. Vance McCarthy, "Strike It Rich!" *Datamation*, February 1997, pp. 45-50.

24. Eva Freeman, "Datamining Unearths Dollars" *Datamation*, July 1997, pp. 84-85.

25. Cheryl Gerber, "Excavate Your Data" *Datamation*, May 1996, pp. 40-43.

26. Deborah Ashbrand, "Is Datamining Ready for the Masses?" *Datamation*, November 1997, pp. 66-71.

27. Vance McCarthy, "Strike It Rich!" *Datamation*, February 1997, pp. 45-50.

28. "Now It's Your Web" *Business Week*, October 5, 1998, pp. 164-178.

Index